Jack the
Ripper's
Streets of
Terror

Jack the Ripper's Streets of Terror

Life during the reign of Victorian London's most brutal killer

Rupert Matthews

This edition published in 2021 by Arcturus Publishing Limited
26/27 Bickels Yard, 151–153 Bermondsey Street,
London SE1 3HA

AD008582UK

Printed in the UK

CONTENTS

INTRODUCTION

THE RIPPER

The serial killer known as Jack the Ripper terrified London for months, brought huge crowds out on to the streets, eluded the police and baffled the medical experts of the time. Even today, nobody is entirely certain how many women Jack the Ripper killed, if he attacked others or how he chose his victims. And he continues to exert a baleful influence over the city he once terrorized. The streets he stalked are today very different, but they still exist. Tour guides usher visitors from murder scene to murder scene, dropping off for a drink in the pubs frequented by the victims – and their killer.

It is not the number of victims that Jack the Ripper claimed that ensure his lasting fame. Only five women were definitely killed by him, and certainly there were no more than eight victims. Other serial killers since then have murdered more. And although the horrific mutilations Jack the Ripper carried out were disturbing and violent, they too have been surpassed since. In the records of serial killers, Jack the Ripper is unexceptional in many ways. But he remains the most famous of them all.

In part this is because he was one of the very first serial killers in the modern sense of the word. In part it was because he was never caught. But largely it was because of the absolute state of terror to which he reduced the greatest city on earth. London was then the most populous city in the world, and the capital of the greatest empire the world had ever seen. Its wealth, sophistication and architecture were famous across the world. Despite the poverty of its East End, London had a water and sewage system so modern that both are still in use today. Street lights illuminated every road, street and alley. The system of law enforcement was the envy of the world.

And yet a sex-crazed serial killer could operate with impunity. Jack the Ripper killed silently, swiftly and apparently at random. But not, it seemed, modestly. Dozens of letters were received by the police and by newspapers. All were followed up, most were hoaxes and at least one person landed in court for wasting police time. But a handful of letters showed detailed knowledge of the crimes. Two were signed 'Jack the Ripper' – giving the faceless murderer a name – and one contained a piece of human kidney apparently taken from one of the victims.

The effect this had on London was shocking, and it is this that has ensured the lasting fame of Jack the Ripper. When one suspect was arrested a crowd of over 2,000 gathered outside the police station to demand that he be sent out for summary justice. Another mob had a rope over a lamppost and some of its members were dragging their victim towards it for a lynching before the police managed to intervene. Men were beaten up for looking at a woman oddly, or dragged to a police station for incarceration simply for being dressed unusually. With terror paralysing the population, anyone could be a suspect – and hundreds were.

The fear and terror that the killer induced forced the police to take the murders seriously. The very best brains that the British police had were sent to Whitechapel to tackle the killer. Hundreds of men were pulled in for detailed questioning, thousands of homes and businesses were searched and street patrols were stepped up. And yet still the killings continued.

The Londoners decided to take things into their own hands. A vigilance committee was set up, funded by local businessmen. Rewards were offered for information, and large numbers of tough men were employed to patrol the streets armed with clubs and pistols. The vigilantes were certainly enthusiastic. Among the men they arrested was a Scotland Yard detective trying to follow up a lead late one evening.

London became a city of horrors, terrors and victims, all dancing to a macabre tune set by a faceless murderer. It became the hunting ground of Jack the Ripper.

CHAPTER 1:

A QUIET YEAR

T he year 1888 was, on the whole, rather quiet. There were no major wars, no big scandals and no large-scale disasters. Britain was reaching the height of its power, influence and industrialized might. This was a time of confidence, prosperity and ever improving conditions for rich and poor alike. Victoria, the Queen–Empress, reigned over a nation that was booming, enjoying democratic reforms and commanding the respect and envy of every nation on earth. Things, it seemed, could only get better.

A TIME OF INCREASING PROSPERITY

The recent history of Britain seemed to indicate that a golden future awaited the country and its inhabitants. As never before people in Britain were involved in international affairs. The upper classes went abroad as colonial governors and administrators. The middle classes went overseas to trade and make money. Even the very poorest went out to see the world, for the soldiers of the Queen marched over six continents in their distinctive red coats. Everywhere the British went they experienced strange and intriguing customs, and were constantly reminded of the material superiority of their own, heavily industrialized country.

On the international stage Britain had been making the running for years. In 1856 the Russian Empire had been defeated in the Crimean War. In 1858 the Indian Mutiny had been put down, the last Indian Emperor dethroned and the British Queen Victoria given the title Empress of India. In 1875 Britain bought the Suez Canal, and effectively took over Egypt to safeguard it. In 1874 the Ashanti Empire of West Africa was overcome and in 1880 the mighty Zulu Empire of southern Africa was destroyed. In 1878 Britain had acted as diplomatic power broker of Europe, forestalling a war between Russia and Austria-Hungary, and had picked up Cyprus by way of reward. All these glories and triumphs were reported in glowing detail in the newspapers and snapped up by an appreciative reading public.

That there was a large and growing market for newspapers was indicative that Britain was enjoying success at home as well as abroad. The levels of literacy in Britain had increased rapidly as cheap education spread. By 1870 around 70 per cent of children were attending school up to the age of about ten. The Forster Education Act of that year set up local School Boards tasked with providing a school place for every child up to the age of 12, to be provided free of charge to poor children. Very quickly attendance rates shot up to over 98 per cent and the vast majority of children were leaving school at the age of 11, able to read, write and do arithmetic to a relatively high standard. By 1888, therefore, most people could read a newspaper without difficulty.

Almost as revolutionary as the ability of the poor to read a newspaper was their ability to buy one. A century earlier it would have been as much as a poor family could do to put food on the table and stop themselves freezing in the winter. A new coat or pair of shoes would have been a rare treat. By 1888, however, a century of industrialization meant that employment was more secure and better paid than it had previously been. An unskilled labourer could expect to be paid four shillings a week, a skilled labourer at least twice that and a foreman supervising others up to 12 or 15 shillings a week. This may not sound much today, but by the standards of previous generations it was fairly good.

As regards costs of living, a good quality house with two bedrooms, front room, kitchen and outside toilet would cost about five shillings a week to rent, a smaller house of similar size around three shillings, a room in someone else's house about one shilling and sixpence, while a bed in a communal dormitory cost a penny a night. A loaf of bread cost a penny, beer threepence a pint and gin around twopence. A skilled labourer could keep himself, a wife and children in a reasonable house and with enough to eat without much difficulty. Even an unskilled worker could manage, especially as children usually went out to work from the age of 11.

Of course, not everyone led a respectable lifestyle. Many were feckless, lazy or took to drink. Others were simply unlucky and fell on hard times through no fault of their own. There was little help available to these 'unfortunates' as they were called. Each local area had a workhouse where free food, lodging and medical care was provided, but everyone tried to avoid the workhouse. The accommodation was very basic, the food was unappetizing and the regime of menial work and curfews was harsh. Sleeping on the street – at least in summer – was preferable to the workhouse for most.

There were many charities providing rather better quality food and lodgings, but they were mostly run by Church authorities that insisted on recipients being both sober and modest. Not everyone who needed help could claim to be both.

For most people in Britain, however, the workhouse was a remote prospect. Most people had jobs and families who would help out in times of need. The year 1888 was, on the whole, a good time to be alive in Britain.

SOME OF THE EVENTS OF 1888

The year opened with a particularly cold snap of bad weather. Snow fell heavily across the country and lakes and canals froze solid, but although this largely closed down the countryside the industrialized cities worked on. That was followed on 9 January by a dense, freezing fog that blanketed the entire country. In London the fog was so bad that a postman fell into a canal and died of cold before he could be fished out. Barges on the river came to a standstill as the steersmen could not see where they were going and by the third day of fog no ships were entering or leaving the port. The magazine *Punch* printed a short verse:

> *King Fog laughed long and loud, and his courtiers, a black crowd,*
> *gathered round their misty Monarch as he cried:*
> *Oh, my henchmen, this is grand. Our strong hand is on the land. We*
> *rule this country, far and wide.*

On the fifth day the fog began to lift, but it was two more days before it was gone completely. The bad weather continued, with ice blocking up the docks and more fog hampering shipping. By the end of January many men working in the docks were suffering financial hardship as the enforced number of days off hit their pay packets. A group of radical politicians called a public meeting, to take place in Trafalgar Square on 8 February, to discuss what steps the government might take to help those who were short of money though they wanted and were willing to work.

All was going well until the socialist Henry Hyndburn got up to speak. Although he came from a wealthy family of industrialist capitalists and had been educated at Eton and Cambridge, Hyndburn had become convinced that socialist revolution was the only way to save mankind. He delivered a firebrand speech that ended: 'Follow me to the West End to demand work, bread or blood.' Part of the crowd did follow him as he set off up Pall Mall, then down St James's towards Buckingham Palace.

As the crowd passed the prestigious Carlton Club one of the gentlemen inside peered out of a window, then held his nose to mock the smell of the working class men surging past. Within seconds every window in the club had been smashed and the mob was hammering at the doors trying to get in. A nearby wine shop was looted, and the already angry throng was further inflamed by drink. The police finally arrived on the scene to make a number of arrests and break up the mob, which dispersed peacefully enough once the blue uniforms were seen.

Hyndburn was charged with inciting a riot and was put on trial at the Old Bailey. The trial turned into a sensation when Hyndburn decided to conduct a defence based on the idea that what he had said in his speech was true. That meant he used the platform of the courtroom to expound his socialist revolutionary views, call witnesses to the economic condition of the poor in London and question experts on politics to support his views. Newspapers serving the poorer areas of London and other big cities covered the trial in great detail. Hyndburn was found not guilty and he left the court in triumph.

The scale of growth in the industrial economy was phenomenal. In 1870 there had been 500 million passenger journeys by rail each year, but by 1890 there were more than 750 million. The amount of freight moved by rail increased even more dramatically. In London the transport crush proved so great that as early as 1863 the underground railways began to be built. By 1888 the Circle Line was complete and it was possible to pass under the City from east to west or north to south by underground railway. Even an impoverished area like Whitechapel was on the underground network, on the line from Shoreditch to New Cross south of the Thames, with another heading west to Baker Street and Holland Park. Coal production had almost tripled between 1850 and 1885, growing from 55 million tons to 145 million tons. Iron and steel production increased just as fast as Britain became the workshop of the world, producing rails and engines to run on them for countries as distant as Australia and Peru.

In March 1888 came news of events both near and far. In India the British Indian Army was ordered to march into the independent state of Sikkim. The Chogyal of Sikkim, Thutob Namgyal, had a treaty of friendship with British India and another with Tibet. In 1886 the Tibetan government had sent a small force of 300 soldiers into Sikkim at the invitation of the chogyal. They built fortifications blocking the road from India into Sikkim, while it was becoming clear that the Tibetans were acting with support and encouragement from China. The British army invaded Sikkim to drive out the Tibetans. The campaign would prove to be arduous due to the mountainous country and terrible roads, but nobody in Britain expected anything other than victory. In fact it would take until 1890 before the Tibetans were ousted and Sikkim reverted to its previous neutral status.

London Bridge was by far the busiest thoroughfare in Britain with 8,000 pedestrian and 900 vehicle movements every hour: some people say that Jack the Ripper used the bridge as his escape route at night.

SENT HOME IN DISGRACE

In the USA the British ambassador got caught up in a scandal that would ultimately lead him to lose his job and be sent home in disgrace. It was election year in the USA and President Grover Cleveland's Republican opponents wanted to undermine his support. They hatched a plan that involved writing letters to assorted public figures, hoping for information they could use. A Mr Charles Murchison of California wrote to British ambassador Sir Lionel Sackville-West claiming to be an English-born American and asking who he should vote for. Sackville-West replied diplomatically and declined to answer the question, though he did include a paragraph stating, 'Mr Cleveland is, I believe, still desirous of maintaining friendly relations with Great Britain.'

The Republicans seized on this section of his reply, publicizing it widely among Irish-Americans and others ill-disposed towards Britain. The ambassador was forced to pack his bags and head home.

Also in March, and significantly closer to home, the Football League was founded. Up until that date it was up to individual clubs to arrange which other clubs they would play and when. As the number of clubs grew this became an increasingly difficult system to administer. The situation was complicated after 1885 when the sport made paying players legal. The bigger clubs quickly hired the best players and naturally wanted to play each other even if they were long distances apart, rather than their much inferior local rivals. A match between two leading clubs would attract crowds of many thousands, generating much greater revenue.

Thus the 12 most popular clubs got together at the suggestion of William McGregor of Aston Villa to form a league. Each club played every other club twice during the season, once at home and once away, with points being awarded depending on if the club won, lost or drew. The first 12 clubs were Accrington, Aston Villa, Blackburn Rovers, Bolton Wanderers, Burnley, Derby County, Everton, Notts County,

Preston North End, Stoke, West Bromwich Albion and Wolverhampton Wanderers. None of these clubs were from London for the simple reason that the London clubs were quite content to play each other and saw no reason to force their fans to travel to Manchester or Birmingham to watch a match. Nevertheless the foundation of the Football League was a major development and the London clubs quickly adopted their own league system of matches and points.

Of rather more interest to Londoners was the eruption on to the music hall stage of a pretty little 17-year-old singer by the name of Marie Lloyd. Born Matilda Wood in Hoxton, London, Lloyd had been on the stage as part of her family singing troupe for years, but she now went solo with what would become her most famous song, 'The Boy I Love Is Up in the Gallery'. The song was perfectly harmless when written down on paper, with its chorus:

> The boy I love is up in the gallery,
> The boy I love is looking now at me,
> There he is, can't you see, waving his handkerchief,
> As merry as a robin that sings on a tree.

But the way young Lloyd sang it, the song was so risqué as to be condemned for being pornographic. With nods, winks and a flick of her skirt Lloyd imbued the song with such sexual innuendo that several theatres were moved to ban her from appearing. When she later tried to take her act to the USA, she was refused entry to the country on the grounds of her 'moral turpitude'. Lloyd was a sensation, packing audiences into London music halls.

At this time there were 78 official music hall theatres in London, with seating capacities varying between 500 and 5,000 paying customers. Lloyd started in the smaller ones, but was soon appearing at the very largest including the Old Bedford in Camden Town and Deacon's at Clerkenwell. These big music halls were fitted out with great luxury, but were not for the upper classes. Even the poorest could afford the occasional penny to occupy the cheap seats up in the gallery from time to time. When King George V visited the Palace Music Hall in 1912 to attend a special charity show put on by the biggest stars of the day it caused a sensation.

In poorer areas, such as Whitechapel, the big stars were unlikely to appear. In fact the majority of music halls in the area were still playing music for people to dance to, as all music halls had originally done. The performers had to compete with vendors selling snacks and drinks for the attention of the crowds. Most music hall evenings ended with dancing by the customers to the strains of the house band. That is not to say the music halls of Whitechapel were small, far from it. One boasted its dance floor could hold 200 dancing couples at one time.

News came from Germany in June that Queen Victoria's grandson had been crowned Kaiser Wilhelm II, ruler of all the German states. Wilhelm was only 29 years old, handsome and dashing with a penchant for military uniforms and a great admiration for his British grandmother. It was widely assumed that the young kaiser would favour friendship with Britain and promote a rapid industrialization of his new realm. Wilhelm set out to do both, and in addition fostered the arts and sciences as no German ruler before him had done. Any tensions between Britain and the Germans were put aside as the new kaiser set out to modernize his empire along British lines.

A DEFEAT FOR SNOBBERY

Meanwhile a school scandal was dominating the newspaper headlines. Some months earlier a 13-year-old boy named Henry Hutt had been expelled from the public school Haileybury, just north of London, for theft. The boy's father, however, refused to accept his son was a thief and sued the school for libel. The trial opened on 10 June to a courtroom packed with reporters eager to discover details of events at the grand school for the children of London's wealthier citizens.

It transpired that there had been a number of petty thefts at the school in the first few months of the year. In an attempt to catch the thief, the proctor, Mr Campbell, secretly marked a number of coins with small scratches then left them lying about the school. It was not long before a couple of the coins went missing. The teachers ordered an immediate search of the premises and one marked half crown was found in the desk of young Hutt. The boy declared he was innocent and that he had no idea how the coin had got into his desk. The headmaster locked Hutt up for three days in an effort to extract a confession, and when the boy continued to plead innocent had him expelled.

Hutt senior was not rich – his son had got into Haileybury on a scholarship – but he was a vicar which meant that he had contacts. He managed to get the case to Charles Russell, son of Lord Russell of Killowen – one of the greatest judges of the Victorian era. Young Charles was trying to make a name for himself and scented in the story a case of snobbery triumphing over evidence. He took on the case, ensuring it even greater publicity than it would otherwise have gathered.

For six full days the court heard details about life at an exclusive school for boys, with the names of several of the greatest families in the land being mentioned and their boys called as witnesses. It was all magnificent gossip for the newspapers, and the tale lost nothing in the telling. Eventually the jury found for the Hutts, ordered the school to pay £100 in damages and further ordered that all school records be changed to make it clear that Hutt was not guilty of theft. A victory for the downtrodden son of an obscure vicar over the authorities of a grand school. The papers, and their readership, loved it.

Another trial caused a brief sensation in the London newspapers when news arrived from Missouri, USA, that a 24-year-old Englishman was due to hang for murder on dubious evidence. Hugh Brooks had been convicted of murdering another Englishman, Lawrence Preller, as the two were travelling across America. The questionable evidence took the form of a statement from a man who had shared Brooks' cell before the trial, in which the man said Brooks had confessed to killing Preller for his money. The cell mate, it transpired, had been paid for the testimony, hence the dispute over its value. What might have been a major story suddenly collapsed when it became clear that other evidence clearly pointed to Brooks being guilty. He was duly hanged.

ALL-OUT STRIKE AT THE MATCH FACTORY

In June the daily life of Londoners was interrupted by an unprecedented industrial action. On 23 June weekly newspaper *The Link* published an article by social reformer Annie Besant deploring working conditions for teenage girls at the Bryant and May match factory in Bow, a mile northeast of Whitechapel. The factory manager wrote a letter to be sent to the newspaper rebutting the story and saying working conditions were good. He went down to the shop floor to ask a worker to sign it. The first girl he approached refused, as did the second and the third. The three girls were sacked on the spot, at which point a great argument broke out about working conditions and within an hour all 1,200 workers at the factory had walked out.

The Matchgirls' Strike, as the event became known, was a major cause célèbre. Victorian society was prone to be sentimental about the treatment of youngsters, while violence against women was increasingly frowned upon. As the truth about conditions at the factory became more widely known, other newspapers and societies took up the cause and public subscriptions were raised to ensure the striking women and girls had enough money to pay for food and rent. Landlords and shop owners extended credit to the strikers, allowing them to pay the bills when they got back to work. Charles Bradlaugh MP, himself an East End boy who had done well in trade, raised the issue in Parliament and invited a group of the girls to meet other MPs. On 16 July the company gave in and agreed to all of the demands over working conditions made by the strikers.

The Matchgirls' Strike caused a sensation across the East End of London. It showed that well organized workers who could get public opinion on their side were able to force concessions from even the most obstinate factory owners. It was, however, an unusual event. Most businesses in London were small, employing only a handful of workers, and very often they were relatives of the business owner. Undoubtedly the strike did have an effect with managers and workers alike recognizing that working conditions should be as safe as reasonably possible.

Parliament was meanwhile rather more concerned with a Commission of Enquiry into what became known as the Phoenix Park letters. In May 1882 the Chief Secretary for Ireland, Lord Cavendish, and his secretary Henry Burke were murdered in Dublin's Phoenix Park by Irish nationalist terrorists, with five men subsequently being convicted and hanged. Early in 1888 a series of letters were published, signed by Charles Parnell MP, leader of the moderate Irish Nationalists in the British Parliament. In the letters Parnell declared his support for the murders and admitted that several members of his political party had taken part in other illegal activity.

Parnell declared the letters were forgeries and that the allegations they contained were entirely untrue and he demanded a Commission of Enquiry. That commission was set up and sat for 128 days, producing a report that ran to 35 bound volumes. The report would not come out until 1889, but when it did it vindicated Parnell completely and named the forger as journalist Richard Pigott.

In July a rather less celebrated, but in the long term no less influential, step was taken. In 1885 a Coventry-based engineering company named Rover produced the first modern bicycle with two small wheels, pedals driving the back wheel via a chain, cable brakes and gears. In 1888 the Scot John Dunlop began selling pneumatic tyres for the Rover bicycle. Suddenly there was a cheap, fast and efficient way for people to get about without the huge expense of a horse. In July Parliament passed a law regulating how bicycles should be ridden on roads, in particular stating that they had to have a bell. The massive upsurge in bicycle ownership and use that would follow caused local councils to improve the surfaces of their roads. In London bicycles were adopted mostly by errand boys and delivery boys, their leisure use being restricted to rural areas and the middle classes. They were rare in poorer areas such as Whitechapel until some years later.

Meanwhile, in August the feminist novelist Mona Caird wrote an article in the *Westminster Review* magazine entitled 'Marriage'. In it she denounced marriage for life as a 'vexatious failure', gave a number of examples of how the law as it stood worked against the interests of women and advocated that the divorce laws should be altered so as to make the separation of married couples – then hugely expensive and almost impossible – much easier to achieve.

The article was followed by a massive outcry that saw newspaper after newspaper printing articles for and against reform of the marriage laws. The public responded to the stories on a massive scale, with the *Daily Telegraph* alone receiving 27,000 letters on the subject. The story and its fall-out were still the main topic of discussion in London newspapers when a gruesome murder in Whitechapel pushed views on marriage off the newspaper agenda.

CHAPTER 2:

THE STREETS OF LONDON

A lthough for the majority of people living in Britain the later 19th century was a time of improving living conditions, better health and welcoming job prospects, there remained pockets of deprivation and poverty that a 21st-century Briton would view with some horror. Rural areas could be blighted by poor harvests and the agricultural economy as a whole was not doing well, but it was in the big cities where the real poverty lay. And no city anywhere was bigger than London.

GROWTH AND POVERTY

In 1888 London had a population of around 6 million souls, making it the biggest city in the world – neither of the next two largest, Paris and New York, were even half as big. London was also the fastest growing city, for in 1800 the population had been about 900,000. As the population boomed the built-up area of London sprawled outwards from the old City to the north, the west, the east and, to a lesser extent, the south. At first the new areas were as densely packed as the old, but then the railways came, making commuting a greater distance more feasible. From the 1860s onwards new suburbs began to be built, featuring houses with gardens and front yards. Inevitably the wealthy and the middle classes moved out to these more salubrious suburbs, leaving the inner city areas increasingly to the poor or to business premises.

Because the prevailing wind in London blows from the west, the smoke from the millions of fires and the smells of millions of people were blown east. The low lying land east of the city was damp, marshy and prone to occasional floods. The housing to the east was therefore cheaper and attracted the poorer members of society. This had long been a feature of London geography, nowhere more noticeably than in the area immediately east of the historic City, that square mile of land within the medieval city walls.

The main road east from the old city walls left at Aldgate, running directly east along the old Roman road to Colchester in Essex. In 1329 a small chapel was built beside the road about half a mile from the city walls. It was dedicated to St Mary, but as it was painted white the locals called it White Chapel. By 1400 there were enough houses clustered along the road for the hamlet of Whitechapel to be given its own parish priest. In 1880 the old chapel burned down and was rebuilt in grand Victorian style. Completed in 1882, it was so large that 1,600 worshippers could be seated at one time amid the mock Gothic splendour of the architecture.

The church was central to life in Whitechapel. Writing in 1891, a visitor recorded:

St. Mary's, Whitechapel, is one of the foremost in popularity and equipment for parish work, and one of the best attended of the great East End churches, everything that may account for its reputation will well deserve attention.

The services are fully choral; the Psalms are chanted both morning and evening, the congregation being led by the surpliced choir. The growing delight in singing as an act of common worship which now characterises all Christian denominations, and which is a great feature of all East London places of worship is indeed amply provided for at St. Mary's.

Sunday evening at St. Mary's is a still larger and more notable demonstration of church-going, and the scene is one of the most encouraging sights which East London can show. The church is filled with at least a thousand persons of the working and poorer classes of Whitechapel. The beautiful and impressive service is an experience not to be forgotten. The sermon, too, is redolent of the place and the people. In the evening the vicar applies himself to the actual circumstances and difficulties of the congregation he knows so well. Here it may be mentioned that the population of the parish is twenty thousand, and that every family of this large number, Jew and Gentile alike, is regularly visited by the rector and his assistant clergy. Mr. Sanders can accordingly put his hand at once on the ills amidst which his people live.

Sunday afternoon is also an occasion for meetings in church for closer dealings with the industrial classes. A gospel address from one of the clergy, the services of an excellent orchestra, reinforced by the fine organ of the church, with popular hymns and sacred solos, attract a class who seldom otherwise see the interior of a beautiful church, or hear sacred music in which they can join, or get into close personal touch with the clergy.

The importance of the parish church at this time was not only spiritual. Much of the social welfare that helped the very poorest in society was channelled through the Church of England. Charitable endowments and local taxes alike flowed through the Church to reach the poor. That centuries-old system was in the process of changing as non-Conformists, Catholics and others combined to overthrow the dominant position of the Church of England.

On 13 August 1888 the Local Government Act passed through Parliament. This created a number of democratically elected county councils which were invested with the administrative and financial powers previously held by the Quarter Sessions so that they could manage their own affairs. Following on from this, in 1889 the entire built-up area of London (except the City itself) was formed into a new county – the County of London – to be administered by the London County Council. That council was responsible for, among other things: raising local taxes, maintaining roads, licensing places of entertainment, providing asylums for lunatics and the sick, controlling contagious diseases, regulating trade and weights, providing schools and maintaining police stations. Whitechapel was one parish of Middlesex that was moved into the new County of London.

LONDON'S POOREST STREETS

By this date, Whitechapel was infamous not only for its poverty, but also for its poor housing and its dangerous streets. Whitechapel High Street and Whitechapel Road, which followed the route of the old Roman road, were themselves quite respectable. They were wide streets frequented by travellers passing through and were lined by shops and businesses of some standing. The narrower streets to the north and south were another matter.

These side streets were narrow and poorly maintained. They were dirty, poorly lit after dark and frequented by the poorest of London's inhabitants. Inevitably the feckless, criminal and mentally weak drifted to this cheap area. People who were dishonest had good reason to stay on the move, drifting from one cheap area to the next, then back again. Some who were not mentally ill enough to warrant being put in an asylum, but who had difficulty holding down a steady job or coping with day to day life, would also end up in cheap areas where landlords did not ask many questions. So too did those who were poor through no fault of their own. Social reformers would decry the way that these 'deserving poor' were forced to live in close proximity to the 'criminal classes' so that they themselves ran the risk of turning to crime.

Dorset Street in Whitechapel was dubbed 'the worst street in London'. There were said to be more petty criminals, prostitutes and drunks here than anywhere else. Even so the honest inhabitants of Whitechapel far outnumbered the criminal. Outsiders might mistake the East Enders' habit of dealing with their own issues as being criminal, but to the local inhabitants it was more a case of keeping things out of the hands of the authorities. Britons of the 19th century did not come into contact much with government. Today we are accustomed to dealing with the government in one form or another on a daily basis – be it paying tax, obeying speed limits on roads, going to a hospital or sending our children to a state school. In 1888 the government was involved in none of these things. People could go their entire lives without paying tax, obeying a regulation or encountering the government in any meaningful way at all.

It was not just the locals who were mostly law-abiding. Many of the people on the streets of Whitechapel did not live there. Cart drivers would enter the area to deliver goods, travellers to or from the City would pass up Whitechapel Road and every day thousands of people walked to work through the streets of Whitechapel. Indeed, far more than today the East End was a society that lived its life out of doors. With no radio, television or internet to keep people occupied at home they would go out to chat to neighbours, take a walk or visit pubs and clubs. At any hour of day or night there were a lot more people walking about Whitechapel in 1888 than is the case now.

AN INFLUX OF IMMIGRANTS

The composition of those people was changing rapidly at this date. The boom in the population of London had always been fuelled by incomers.

Throughout the Middle Ages and well into the 17th century the bulk of those moving to London were country folk from elsewhere in England. By 1521 working class Londoners were being referred to by the rural residents of counties near the city as 'cockneys'. This was something of an insult as the word then had a general meaning of a weakling. By 1660 Londoners were using the name to refer to themselves. By the 1820s the word meant a native Londoner 'born within the sound of Bow bells', in contrast to a newcomer to the city. By that date many of the incomers to London were not English at all, but Welsh, Irish or Scottish. Those earlier waves of immigrants to London had been absorbed, on the whole, peacefully and completely but by the 1880s changes were taking place.

In 1881 Tsar Alexander II of Russia was murdered by a group of left-wing revolutionaries. A wave of anti-Jewish pogroms followed as loyal Tsarists blamed the Jews for the underlying revolutionary feelings – one of the conspirators having been Jewish. Although the members of the wider Jewish community were innocent, waves of riots and civil disorder swept the western provinces of the Russian Empire – mostly Poland, Ukraine and Belorussia. Only a handful of Jews were killed, but hundreds of houses, synagogues and businesses were burned while thousands suffered beatings and injuries. In the months and years that followed, tens of thousands of Jews fled the Russian Empire. Some went to Germany, others to the USA, but a large number came to Britain. Attracted by the cheap housing and the fact that few questions were asked, many of them went to the East End of London. By 1888 there were around 80,000 Jews in London.

Unlike earlier waves of immigrants to London, the Russian Jews spoke a different language, had a different religion and dressed in strange ways. Moreover, they did not adopt the customs and dress of the native Londoners as the earlier immigrants had done, so they stuck out like a sore thumb on the streets. The native Londoners proved to be wary of these new arrivals with their strange habits and foreign customs, and their habit of sticking together instead of mixing with neighbours. To call this suspicion and wariness anti-Semitism would be to overstate the case, but there was certainly an undercurrent of mistrust.

It was not just the native Londoners who were concerned. The members of the long-established Jewish community in London were also getting concerned. They thought that the new arrivals might spark anti-Semitism by their refusal to assimilate into English culture. Lord Rothschild, one of the richest and most influential Jews in England, wrote: 'We have now a new Poland on our hands in east London. Our first business is to humanize our Jewish immigrants and then to Anglicize them.' There had been no anti-Semitic violence and little real trouble, but many people in authority were concerned about the building tension and worried that trouble would flare up in the near future.

LIFE IN THE LODGING HOUSES

Most of the houses in Whitechapel dated from the late 18th century or the early 19th century. The majority had been built to be single residences, usually with a shop or workroom occupying the ground floor, but over the years they had been divided up into separate dwellings. More recent houses were built with this subdivision in mind. Most such houses had a front door that was unlocked at most times so that anyone could walk in. The front door gave access to a staircase that had a sizeable landing on each floor. Off that landing were doors leading to the individual dwellings. Some might occupy an entire floor, others just a single room. Sometimes the rooms were rented out by a landlord who lived in the house itself; at other times the landlord lived miles away and sent an agent to collect the rents. Vagrants and the destitute would often seek shelter in the open corridors and landings, while the residents would seek to chase out those who caused trouble – mostly the drunks.

Drunks were also a problem lower down the housing scale. Those who could not afford permanent lodgings, or were in town for only a few days, frequented what were known as common lodging houses. Although these houses varied greatly in comfort and respectability, they did conform to a standard pattern. Entrance was gained by a single door opening on to the street. That door gave access to a narrow passage that was overlooked by a small office which had a window and a counter. The warden of the house occupied the office, taking a fee of threepence or fourpence from each person entering for the night. The warden, or manager, might also sell food to occupants.

PRECARIOUS CIRCUMSTANCES

The ground floor was largely taken up by a kitchen and dining area. Anyone staying overnight was free to use the stove and range to cook food or to sit in the kitchen. Many warders would allow non-residents to use the kitchen, especially if they were known to each other. However, all non-residents were usually turned out by midnight. If someone did not have the threepence or fourpence needed to pay for a bed they would have to sleep rough. Also on the ground floor, at least in the better houses, was a bathroom or two where for an extra penny a resident could take a bath.

Upstairs the lodging house was divided into a number of dormitories which contained rows of bunk beds. In theory the bedding was washed each day, but in the less reputable and cheaper houses this could not be guaranteed. There was little or no privacy in these rooms, so most people slept fully or partially clothed. Most lodging houses had separate rooms for men and women, with small rooms for families. Others did not segregate the sexes and a few tolerated men and women sharing beds without checking if they were married or even claimed to be.

Many of the people using common lodging houses were only moving through London. Sailors were frequent customers as were itinerant tradesmen or other people in London for a few days who were short of money. Of the locals, only the poorest slept regularly in lodging houses. Anyone with claims to respectability would seek a room rented by the week. Even the poorest did not always sleep in the lodging houses. During the summer a bench by the river or in a park would do, and would be free of charge. When winter closed in, however, the streets were less welcoming.

Whether a house was a single dwelling, divided into flats or a common lodging house it would have an outside toilet at the back. Until the middle of the century, these toilets had consisted of a seat positioned over a large wooden box. Once a week or so a man came with a pony and cart into which he emptied the contents of the box to be taken away.

The stinking contents had a value as fertilizer once they had rotted down and, if the urine was kept separate, it could be sold to leather tanners and other industries. However, the presence of large quantities of human excrement had caused increasing health problems.

In the 1860s the specially established Metropolitan Board of Works had dug about 75 miles of main sewers and 1,000 miles of street sewers to collect sewage from London and pump it east to Beckton, where it was dumped into the Thames Estuary safely downriver of London.

The sewage was later crudely treated before being put into the river. Nevertheless, the extensive sewage works dramatically improved the health of all Londoners, even the poorest. Waterborne diseases such as cholera and dysentery vanished almost overnight.

THE PROBLEM OF ALCOHOL

Drink was a real problem in Whitechapel in the 1880s, but many saw it as being as much a symptom as a cause of the social ills of the East End of London. Beer, gin and whisky were cheap and easy to get hold of. In 1869 a new law came in that required anyone selling alcoholic drinks to have a licence to do so issued by the local magistrates. The licences were difficult to obtain and usually came with all sorts of conditions attached. These conditions were rigorously enforced by the local police, and most licensees stuck to the terms of their licence. In London, licences tended to restrict the selling of alcohol to specific locations and specific hours. Landlords were not allowed to serve someone who was already clearly drunk or disorderly, nor were they allowed to have prostitutes or gambling on the premises. Music or other entertainment was not generally allowed, though there were some special exemptions.

Entertainment usually took place in separate buildings that were not allowed to sell alcohol. Dance halls and music halls were the most numerous of these in the East End, but a scattering of theatres put on proper plays.

The pub, short for public house, that dominated the selling of alcohol, could be a highly varied institution. Some took the form of genuine houses open to the public, but most were larger and grander structures built specifically for the purpose. There tended to be two bars. The public bar was simple, plain and spartan. All surfaces were designed to be easily cleaned for it was here that workers came at lunchtime or on their way home from work, when they were in overalls covered in grease, dust or other dirt.

Adjacent was the lounge or saloon where the same people would go in the evening when they had changed out of their dirty work clothes into clean outfits. These bars had padded, upholstered seats, carpets, cut glass lights and other luxuries that the poorer people could not afford at home. Women did not tend to go into the public bar at all, and respectable women would not go into the saloon bar alone. Women accompanied by a brother, husband or boyfriend would very often be seen in saloon bars.

The landlords of some pubs tolerated the presence of prostitutes so long as they took any customers away from the pub before indulging in sex.

Despite the prohibition on serving a person already drunk, heavy drinking was common. Some found in drinking a release from the daily grind of work and poverty, others simply enjoyed getting drunk – and still others were addicted to alcohol. Although landlords and their staff usually kept order inside pubs, the streets were a different matter. Even people who were not drunk could be the worse for drink, and there has always been a minority of people who turn violently aggressive when drinking – what used to be termed 'fighting drunk'. With large numbers of people, many of them having drunk at least some alcohol, walking around the streets of an evening, Whitechapel could be an intimidating place.

Saturday night was the big social evening out for the East End. Most workers had Sunday off, and the majority of manual workers were paid in cash as they left work on Saturdays. Most people got involved in nothing more serious than boisterous singing or ribald remarks directed at passers-by, but fights were not uncommon. These mostly took the form of punch-ups between two men and ended when one of the men went down. A fight would attract a crowd of passers-by eager to see the action, and since most would know at least one of the protagonists the crowd members would often take sides.

WIDESPREAD VIOLENCE

Although violence was much more common in Whitechapel in 1888 than in any part of Britain today, it was neither random nor out of control. Local custom and culture set clear limits on what was acceptable. The use of knives or guns was frowned upon, and if a man produced one he was as likely as not to be swiftly disarmed by the crowd around him.

Kicking a man when he was down was equally unacceptable, though some especially vicious types would get one kick in before accepting victory and moving off. Such fights were common. One gentleman who was obliged to live in Whitechapel for several weeks in 1886 later recorded that he saw at least one street fight every Saturday night, and on average two others during the week.

Murder, even an accidental killing in a fight, was not only frowned upon but was rare. In 1887 there was only one murder in Whitechapel, and in 1889 none at all. So while violence was common and widespread, killing was not. One reason for this will have been the death penalty which hovered over anyone engaged in crime. At this date killing a person 'by accident' when engaged in robbery or burglary was counted as wilful murder and simply taking a weapon when engaged in crime was tantamount to attempted murder. Even a drunken man engaged in a street fight would know that the noose would be his end if he killed the man he was fighting. Everyone else knew this too, so they tended to intervene if it looked as if one participant had had enough.

It was not just the severity of the punishment that deterred violence from turning fatal. There was also the near certainty of getting caught. East Enders famously dealt with their own problems, with local men of influence ordering beatings to be administered to those who misbehaved. But the police were far more integrated into the local community then than is the case today. Few people in 21st-century London could name a policeman, but in 1888 everyone could.

POLICING CRIME

The Metropolitan Police Force had been founded in 1829 to replace the old system of voluntary parish constables, which was getting overwhelmed by the massive growth in population. At its beginnings, and still in 1888, the prime job of the Met, as it became known, was to enforce law and order on the streets. The key tool to achieve this was the police constable on his beat.

Policemen were paid a basic weekly wage of one guinea, a gold coin worth one pound and one shilling. This was a relatively high rate of pay at the time, higher even than the going rate for a foreman in a skilled industry. Constables had to be under the age of 35 when recruited and needed to be able to read and write, to be physically fit, to stand over 5 feet 7 inches tall and to be of unblemished honesty, reputation and character. They were put into a uniform of dark blue wool able to withstand the worst of British weather, with a toughened hat that not only kept off rain and sun but was proof against fists, bottles or clubs. To help him keep order each policeman had a wooden truncheon to use in fights or when subduing a suspect, plus a whistle to summon assistance from other policemen if a situation looked likely to get out of hand.

Thus equipped the policeman went out on his beat. The beat was an area of London around which a policeman could walk in less than an hour, going up every street, looking into every yard or alley and chatting to shopkeepers or passers-by. The policeman was expected to be on duty 12 hours a day, six days a week. He had to know by sight everyone who lived or worked on his beat, and by name anyone who was of importance for good or bad reasons. He was expected to know who was a pickpocket, who was a burglar and who could be relied on to help in a crisis. He had to be familiar with trouble spots, be aware of when fights might break out and be able to deal with them.

The mere appearance of a policeman on the spot was often enough to stop fights or other trouble instantly. Most policemen were big, burly and backed by the full force of the law. Like others in the East End, beat policemen were accustomed to dealing with problems themselves rather than calling in higher authorities. A thwack with a truncheon would

A police constable on the beat uses his bull's eye lantern to inspect a shop window for signs of disturbance.

teach a quick, sharp lesson that could be far more effective than hauling someone up before the magistrates. If any policeman was tempted to abuse his position, he had his sergeant to answer to – and sergeants were expected to be almost as familiar with what went on in their area as a constable was with events on his beat.

The beats of the constables were carefully designed. Not only were they laid out so that each street had a policeman walking down it about once an hour, but they intersected with each other. It was usual for a policeman on his beat to wait at the intersection point for the man patrolling the next beat to turn up. This allowed them to compare notes on what was going on, but also to check all was well. If a policeman did not turn up after a while his colleague would go looking for him.

Similarly the beats were arranged so that each man was within range of the whistle of his colleague on a neighbouring beat. In the days before motorized traffic and other noisy modern machinery a police whistle blown at full blast could carry a surprising distance. So dense on the ground were policemen on patrol at this date that the first reaction of anyone discovering a crime was to shout or run to the nearest main road – knowing full well that a policeman would be along in a minute or two. It was a system designed to keep order on the streets. And, by and large, it worked. Street fights may have been commonplace, but they rarely lasted long before they were broken up by the arrival of a policeman. Likewise disputes and arguments were quickly calmed by the arrival of a man in a blue uniform.

THE LONG ARM OF THE LAW

Anyone intending to commit a crime did so in the full and certain knowledge that before long a policeman would come walking by. A broken window, a door forced open or any other sign of something amiss would attract the attention of a policeman walking past who was accustomed to how things should look. Burglars knew they had to work quickly, quietly and with great care if they were not to be caught. Pickpockets had to be able to escape quickly, either melting into a crowd or running off down a side street or an alley at high speed.

It was not just the police who were on the lookout for criminals. London also had several thousand 'vigilants' – privately employed security guards. Most of these men were hired to patrol upmarket residential streets – of which there were none in Whitechapel – or commercial premises – of which there were many. These vigilants were sometimes more heavily armed than were the police – swords were commonplace and pistols not entirely unknown. They might patrol the buildings or streets they were hired to protect, or they might have a vantage point where they could sit and rest while keeping an eye on things. Unlike the police, the vigilants were not supposed to get involved in punch-ups or anything that did not directly threaten what they were guarding, but they did tend to keep an eye open for anything unusual. A policeman on his beat would make a point of stopping to talk to the vigilants he passed, both to check they were awake and doing their jobs and to ask if anything untoward had occurred.

In 1877 the Criminal Investigation Department (CID) was introduced. This branch of the Met was composed of detectives who would be called in to investigate crimes, detect who was responsible and bring them to justice. The tools available to a detective of the CID in 1888 were primitive by modern standards – there was no system of fingerprinting, establishing blood groups or analyzing fibres or other trace materials, never mind the studying of DNA or other high-tech facilities.

But that is not to say that a CID detective was wholly powerless. By 1888 the Met had a range of facilities and procedures at its disposal. If a constable came across the scene of a crime he was under orders to secure it to stop passers-by interfering with evidence before a detective arrived. The detective would begin with a careful search of the scene for clues. These might take the form of footprints (allowing the footwear used by a criminal to be established), scraps of cloth, the marks of tools used by the criminal, objects dropped by the criminal, or taken by him. Having searched the scene, the detective would move on to question in detail anyone linked to the crime or its scene in any way. Meanwhile, teams of constables would fan out to call on nearby properties armed with a list of questions compiled by the detective. The responses given would be recorded and passed on to the detective, who would then go and interview anybody who gave answers of interest.

This system of looking for clues, door-to-door enquiries and detailed questioning of anyone involved would be familiar to detectives today. The tools and equipment may have become more sophisticated, but the basic methodology of detective work has not changed much. Nor has the role of a detective's instinct for when something is wrong or not quite right. More than once, culprits have first attracted attention to themselves by responding oddly to a routine question.

The policemen who had the unenviable job of trying to track down Jack the Ripper were not as helpless as may be supposed. The Met of the 1880s had a good record of solving crimes and bringing culprits to justice. But then they were used to crimes such as the murder of a work colleague or a family member for reasons such as greed, a private grudge or jealousy. With Jack the Ripper they would be dealing with something new and infinitely more terrible: the world's first serial killer.

CHAPTER 3:

VIOLENCE AGAINST WOMEN

During the course of the 19th century the status of women in society was rising, and the way women were treated was changing. The past was being left behind, but never for a moment forgotten. These changes were affecting how women were treated not just by men but by other women. Given that Jack the Ripper specialized in brutal violence against women, the reaction of society to his crimes was a good indicator of how women were viewed.

THE RISE OF SOCIAL LEGISLATION

Three basic changes affecting women were taking place in the 19th century and were driving the changes to how women were seen and treated. The first was legal, the second was economic and the third social.

In the legal sphere the state was becoming more and more interested in what its citizens got up to. In part this was because the growing state wanted to tax people, but also there was a perceived need for the state to save people from themselves and from others. Before about 1790 the criminal law as enforced by the state was concerned with outlawing crimes such as theft, fraud, murder and rape. Other matters, such as employment, the quality of goods in shops and marriage were considered to be no business of the government at all. Those matters were left to the individuals to sort out for themselves, backed by civil law if necessary. The attitude was that if you did not like working at one factory you should go and get a job somewhere else, if you did not like the bread sold in one baker's shop then you should buy your bread from somebody else.

As the 19th century progressed, that attitude changed. Social reformers argued that if all factories offered bad working conditions the worker had no choice but to accept them, and if all bakers in a town sold bad bread then the residents had no choice but to buy it. In particular it was argued that the more vulnerable members of society – the poor, children and women – were not able to look after themselves. Thus was born social reform legislation.

The Factory Act of 1802 banned the employment of children under the age of nine, and restricted those aged nine to 13 to working only eight hours a day. Factory owners were also obliged to give their child workers two suits of new clothes a year and provide an hour of Christian education each Sunday. Subsequent Acts brought in rules on the employment of women, including a maximum working day of 12 hours, an obligatory one-hour break for lunch, no work on Sundays and the twice-yearly washing and disinfecting of working rooms. In 1878 all this legislation was rolled together into the 1878 Factory Act, a comprehensive work that sought to make employment safer and more comfortable for all women and children working in factories or workshops.

At the same date the state was involving itself in food safety. Traditionally every rural family had what today would be considered a smallholding on which to grow fruit and vegetables and to keep some chickens and a pig or a cow. When the population moved into cities this was no longer possible. People had to buy all their food from shops, whose owners were sometimes less than honest.

From about 1820 doctors had started to get concerned that some substances used to colour foods – for instance lead to make cheese yellow – might be injurious to health. They had little evidence to support them until the 1850s when new chemical understanding backed them up.

Fortunately the common people were already reacting against what was termed the adulteration of food. As early as 1780 a miller was found to have been adding chalk to flour to make it whiter. At that date there was no law against this, but a sudden drop in sales caused him to change his ways. In 1860 the Food and Drink Adulteration Act not only outlawed the use of a wide range of chemicals and substances, but also obliged local authorities to investigate and prosecute complaints.

WOMEN AND CHILDREN FIRST

The new laws that specifically affected women were part of this new mood of state involvement in private lives. In 1853 the issue of domestic violence was tackled for the first time. Before this there had been a general attitude that it was up to the male head of the household to enforce good standards of behaviour on his family. If, for instance, a child was rude to someone he would be taken home for his father to apply punishment. In the stable, rural societies common before industrialization this system had worked well enough. Everyone in a village knew everyone else and nobody wanted a reputation for either a lax attitude to social norms or for being unnecessarily brutal. There was real pressure on men to enforce good behaviour, but not to be too harsh about it.

In cities, these social pressures did not operate. Male heads of household were more likely to lose control of family members as young men increasingly lived alone. At the same time those men who were naturally violent, or were so after drink, had few constraints on their viciousness. Outsiders were reluctant to interfere in what a man did in his own home. In 1853 that changed with the Act for the Better Prevention and Punishment of Aggravated Assaults upon Women and Children. This did not stop the physical chastisement of women and children by the male head of the household, but it did make it clear that anything that would be considered a crime if committed on a stranger would be considered a crime within the family.

It was not just that the government was increasingly getting interested in people's behaviour – the industrial revolution was having an impact on women's lives. In rural communities young women usually stayed in their family home until they married and set up a home with their new husband. However in an industrialized society it was perfectly possible for a young woman to go out to work and earn a wage for herself. This gave young women money of their own in their pocket to spend. While upper and middle class families frowned on their adult daughters behaving in this way, working class families were rapidly coming to terms with theirs having money and wanting to spend it.

Not only did young women go out to work in factories or workshops. Once they were married and had children of their own, women would take in piece work. This was very often work that required dextrous, nimble fingers rather than masculine brawn. Married women would do laundry, ironing, knitting or sewing at home. They were paid according to how much work they had managed to get done when not looking after their family tasks. This provided married women with a source of cash income independent of their husbands, and with the money came the desire and ability to spend it. Women were becoming increasingly independent because they had the money to be so.

By the 1880s it was becoming perfectly normal for working class women to go out in pairs or small groups to visit the music hall or a social club, or simply to visit each other's houses for a cup of tea and a chat. There were concerns that women out alone might be vulnerable to men – especially those with muscles hardened by physical work in mines or factories. It rapidly became frowned upon for men to be physically violent towards women. Just as important it became the duty of all decent men to stand up for a woman in such a situation.

This was part of a growing mood that violence against women and children was unacceptable and, moreover, that men had to behave in a selfless manner when dealing with them. In 1889 a journalist from an upmarket West End newspaper wrote a piece about an expedition to the East End. Among other scenes he gave prominence to the following incident:

There was one very sad sight I witnessed at Globe Road, where a dozen or so persons had assembled. A young girl, who certainly had not attained to her eighteenth year, was carrying a sickly infant in her arms. A finely built young fellow, who was considerably the worse for liquor, and who was apparently the husband of the girl, was entreated by the latter to come home. Muttering some inaudible sentence, this fine young fellow, without the slightest provocation, struck his wife a cowardly blow, and then offered to fight any one of the bystanders. This was more than mortal man could bear, and one burly-looking individual roughly seized him by the neck and proceeded to march him in the direction of home.

It is worth noting, in passing, that nobody thought to call the police. This was the sort of thing that the local community dealt with itself, whatever the growing mass of social legislation might say.

In 1887 another incident took place far from Whitechapel that also showed the prevailing opinion that women and children deserved special treatment. Late on the afternoon of 19 May the passenger liner SS *Britannic* with 450 passengers and 175 crew on board was pushing slowly through dense fog off the coast of New Jersey. Looming suddenly out of the fog at high speed came the SS *Celtic* which rammed the *Britannic* in the stern, tearing open a great gash and allowing the sea water to flood in. The captain gave the order to abandon ship, hailing the *Celtic* to stand by to receive his passengers and crew. It was usual by this date for women and children, considered less likely to survive in the water, to be given precedence in the lifeboats.

At this point the ship gave a lurch and seemed about to go down quickly. Several men rushed to get into the lifeboats, pushing the women and children aside. The captain pushed his way to the front of the crowd, produced a pistol and pointed it straight at a man's head. 'I will kill the first man to get into a lifeboat,' he called in a clear, loud voice. The move calmed the crowd, allowing the boats to be filled with the women and children who were taken to the *Celtic* before the boats came back for the men. It was then found that the *Britannic* was not sinking, so the crew stayed on board and took her slowly to New York. Interestingly one of the officers on board *Britannic* was one Edward Smith who in 1912 would be captain of the RMS *Titanic* and who again would forcefully insist on a women and children first policy.

ATTACKS ON WOMEN IN THE YEAR BEFORE THE TERROR

The 'Rainham Mystery'

Violence against women was becoming increasingly socially unacceptable as the status of women increased. The social pressure on men of all classes to treat women with respect and dignity was strong and growing. But lurking under that social insistence was a very real appreciation of the fact that most men are physically stronger than most women and that some men were vicious and abusive. Women could be in real danger, and it was to counter this that the social norms were brought into play.

That violence against women did take place was brought forcefully home to the citizens of London in May 1887. A man walking beside the Thames at Rainham spotted a bundle wrapped in rags that was bobbing low in the water. He hooked it ashore, perhaps thinking it might be something lost off a ship that he could sell. But when he unwrapped the rags he found the naked torso of a woman, missing its limbs and head. He at once called the police, who took the body off to a mortuary. In the days that followed several more packets containing body parts were pulled from the river until police had the entire body, apart from the head.

The police called in Dr Thomas Bond who studied the remains. He came to the conclusion that the body had been dismembered by somebody with some knowledge of anatomy, but not necessarily by a doctor. A butcher or a knacker would have possessed the necessary skills. It proved to be impossible to identify the victim, and nobody was reported missing. With little to go on the police wrote off the 'Rainham Mystery' as insoluble.

Annie Millwood

It was not only the murder of women that attracted attention – so did assaults. These were surprisingly rare in London at this date, most fights being between men, and when they did occur they were either domestic in nature or between rival matriarchs. On 7 April 1888 the *East London Advertiser* carried a story about a violent attack on a woman. It seems to have attracted press attention as the woman subsequently died.

Annie Millwood was 38 years old and desperately poor, though as the widow of a soldier she would have been receiving a small pension. She was a perfectly honest and respectable woman who was out for an evening somewhere, perhaps a pub or a music hall. At about half past one in the morning on 25 February she was brought to the door of the Whitechapel Infirmary by a man who, having deposited her, went away. He seems to have been a passer-by who lent a hand.

Millwood was found to be suffering from numerous stab wounds to her stomach and thighs. The police were summoned, but Millwood could not tell them much. She had been walking down the road when a man whom she did not know accosted her. Thinking he was asking for directions or something similar, Millwood stopped. The man then pulled a clasp knife from his pocket and stabbed her a number of times before running off. She was then helped to the hospital. Although she was seriously wounded, Millwood made a complete recovery. The location of the attack was not recorded, though as Millwood was taken to the Whitechapel Infirmary it must have taken place nearby.

On 21 March Millwood was released from hospital into the care of the Whitechapel Workhouse. The workhouse stood on what was then Charles Street (now Vallance Road) just north of Whitechapel Road. Millwood was still poorly and unable to work, so a spell in the workhouse where she would be assured of food and shelter was thought the best option. Ten days later Millwood was in the backyard of the workhouse when, in the words of Richard Sage, employed at the workhouse as a messenger,

About 11:40 a.m. on the 31st ult., I was standing at the door conversing with the deceased, and my attention being called in another direction I turned my back to her, and after a space of three minutes I returned, to find her lying down with her face on the step. I acquainted the porter, who had her carried into the corridor.

The tale was then taken up by Thomas Badcock, Master of the Workhouse.

On Saturday the 31st ult., my attention was drawn to her as she was then laying down in the corridor, apparently in a fit. I immediately telephoned to the infirmary for medical aid, and finding the case

to be one of great urgency I procured the services of Dr. Wheeler,
of Mile End-road, who came at once and pronounced life to be
extinct. Dr. Arthur arrived shortly afterwards from the infirmary,
and corroborated Dr. Wheeler, and I then placed her in a shell,
and sent the body to the mortuary. She had never complained
of feeling unwell, but on the other hand she seemed always in
excellent spirits.

The doctors soon found that she had died when her left pulmonary artery
ruptured due to an ulcer. The death had nothing to do with the stabbing,
though that cannot have helped her overall health.

There were a few features about the attack on Millwood that would
have struck contemporaries as rather unusual. Most attacks in the street
were the result of either a dispute, often fuelled by alcohol, or of robbery.
The man who attacked Millwood neither had an argument with her first
nor did he seek to rob her. He simply stabbed her several times and then
ran off. This was very odd behaviour in London at the time.

Ada Wilson

Another peculiar assault on a woman hit the headlines in the East End
in April. The story was covered by the *East London Advertiser*, the *East
London Observer* and the *Eastern Press*. Clearly this was a story of great
interest in east London, but not to outsiders. The victim this time was
Ada Wilson, who lived and worked as a dressmaker at 19 Maidman
Street, which was in Mile End, almost a mile east of Whitechapel proper.
Ada was married, but there is some confusion as to whether she lived
with her husband or not. In any case she occupied the ground floor of the
two-storey house. The upper floor of the house was occupied by 24-year-
old Rose Bierman and her mother. The two tenants did not have much

to do with each other and seem to have been on merely nodding terms with each other.

The accounts of Ada and Rose differ as to precisely what happened. According to Ada it was just gone midnight when the drama began. The *East London Observer* recorded her account as follows:

> She was about to retire to rest when she heard a knock at the door, and upon going there found a total stranger waiting, who demanded money, adding that if she did not at once produce the cash she had but a few moments to live. She refused to give the money and the man at once drew from his pocket a clasp knife, with which he stabbed her twice in the throat. From the details of the man's appearance given by Wilson, the following will be found a fairly accurate description of the man:– Aged about 30, height 5 ft. 6 in.; face sunburnt, with fair moustache; dressed in dark coat, light trousers, and wideawake hat. Detective-Inspectors Wildey and Dillworth are looking for him. It is thought impossible that the injured woman can recover.

It should be noted that the door referred to here was the inner door that gave access to Wilson's rooms from the passage running from the front door to the stairs up to the Bierman rooms on the top floor.

The slightly different account given by Rose Bierman appeared around the same time in the *Eastern Post*.

> Ada Wilson, the injured woman, is the occupier of the house, but at the time of the outrage she was under notice to quit. I knew Mrs. Wilson as a married woman, although I had never seen her husband. Last evening she came into the house accompanied by a male companion, but whether he was her husband or not I could not

say. She has often had visitors to see her, but I have rarely seen them myself, as Mrs. Wilson lives in the front room, her bedroom being just at the back, adjoining the parlour. My mother and I occupy two rooms upstairs. Well, I don't know who the young man was, but about midnight I heard the most terrible screams one can imagine. Running downstairs I saw Mrs. Wilson, partially dressed, wringing her hands and crying, 'Stop that man for cutting my throat! He has stabbed me!' She then fell fainting in the passage. I saw all that as I was coming downstairs, but as soon as I commenced to descend I noticed a young fair man rush to the front door and let himself out. He did not seem somehow to unfasten the catch as if he had been accustomed to do so before. He had a light coat on, I believe. I don't know what kind of wound Mrs. Wilson has received, but it must have been deep, I should say, from the quantity of blood in the passage. I do not know what I shall do myself. I am now 'keeping the feast', and how can I do so with what has occurred here? I am now going to remove to other lodgings.

The reference made by Rose Bierman to 'keeping the feast' refers to the Passover as she and her mother were Jewish. There are some other points worth noting in her account. First she implies that Ada Wilson may not have lived with her husband, but nevertheless had numerous visitors at least some of whom were male. This would have raised a few eyebrows among contemporary readers. The implication was that Ada Wilson was a prostitute, or perhaps a mistress to a married man. If this were the case it might explain why Rose Bierman did not have much to do with her socially. Ada Wilson herself gave her profession as dressmaker, and there were plenty of women earning a living with needle and thread who worked at home. However, it is possible that Wilson gave this as her profession to explain why she stayed at home and did not go out to work.

However Ada earned her living Rose Bierman implies that the man who attacked Ada Wilson was the same man with whom she came home some time earlier. By Rose's account then Ada Wilson was a prostitute who was attacked by a client, perhaps in a dispute over money. Ada herself claimed to be a respectable woman attacked by a total stranger. Both might have had reasons to give different versions. If Wilson had been a prostitute she may have been seeking to cover up this fact. If she had not been, perhaps Bierman was seeking to smear the reputation of a neighbour she did not much like.

The press reports do agree about what happened after the young man with fair hair, moustache and sunburned face had fled the house in Maidman Street. Rose Bierman ran out of the house screaming and shrieking at the top of her voice. This roused a woman neighbour who came out to see what was happening. Together the two women then ran to Burdett Road, the nearest main road, where they found two policemen outside the Royal Hotel. The policemen ran with the two women back to the house where they found Ada Wilson prostrate in the passageway and bleeding heavily. While one policeman applied rough first aid the other sped off to find a doctor. Since he was on his own beat, the policeman knew the address of all the local doctors and within minutes had returned with a doctor who bound up the neck wounds. Wilson was then taken to hospital where next morning she had recovered enough to give her version of events to the police.

Ada Wilson recovered slowly, leaving the hospital a couple of weeks later. What happened to her after that is unknown. Once her role as victim in a savage assault was over she was of no further interest to either the newspapers or the police. She might be the Ada Wilson recorded in the 1891 census as living in Salter Street, Limehouse, the eldest of five children of Robert and Charlotte Wilson. On the other hand she may have been a quite different Ada Wilson who by 1891 had left the East End.

Her assailant similarly vanished from sight. The descriptions given by Wilson and Bierman were fairly clear, but frustratingly vague. There must have been many men in London about 30 years of age and 5ft 6ins in height, with a sunburnt face and a fair moustache, who wore a dark coat and light trousers with a wide-brimmed hat. At any rate the police were unable to find anyone in the vicinity who matched the description nor anyone who knew who it might be.

Emma Smith

Only a few days later another assault on a woman would lead to death. This time it was the *Eastern Post* that was first to report the incident on 7 April, under the heading of 'FATAL STABBING CASE IN WHITECHAPEL'. The story gave few details other than that a widow named Emma Smith had died after being attacked in the street late on the night of Easter Monday, 3 April. Other newspaper reports over the following days added more details.

Emma Smith was not actually a widow but she was estranged from her husband whom she had left in 1877. She had a son who lived in Finsbury Park who is thought to have sent money to her from time to time. However, Smith mostly earned her living as a prostitute. For the two years before her death she had lived almost full time in a common lodging house at 18 George Street, just off Commercial Road in Whitechapel. The lodging house was run by a Mrs Mary Russell who was on good terms with Smith and although she knew of Smith's profession did not object so long as nothing untoward happened on the premises.

Among her friends and neighbours, Smith had a mixed reputation. She was generally thought to have come from a good family, but had fallen on hard times. She was also well known as a tough woman who resorted to her fists when she had been drinking or if she thought another prostitute was infringing on her favoured working areas.

Her daily routine was firm and rarely varied. If she was working, she would leave George Street at about 7 pm and walk east to Limehouse. There she would ply her trade on the street until about 2 am when she returned home to the lodging house. She would then sleep until morning when she would spend the day chatting and drinking with friends. On nights when she was not working, she would remain in the lodging house all night.

On the evening of Monday 2 April she had gone out as usual. Another prostitute who knew her well, Margaret Hayes, saw her some time after midnight on the corner of Farrant Street and Burdett Road talking to a man she took to be a client. Knowing how Smith was likely to react if she thought Hayes was trying to poach a client, Hayes gave the couple a wide berth.

The next person to see Smith was Mary Russell. At about 3 am Smith arrived back in George Street in a terrible condition. Her face was battered, her ear was torn and bleeding and she was holding her shawl to her groin from which heavy bleeding was coming. Smith managed to blurt out that she had been attacked and robbed before she collapsed. The police were summoned, but Russell did not wait for them to arrive. She roused a lodger named Annie Lee and together they carried Smith to the London Hospital on Whitechapel Road. She was treated by the surgeon on duty, George Haslip, and remained conscious long enough to give a brief description of what had happened. She then became unconscious and died on the Wednesday without recovering consciousness.

According to Smith she had been walking home when, near Whitechapel Church, she had seen a group of four men coming towards her. Not liking the look of the men, one of whom was a fresh-faced youth of about 19, she crossed the road to avoid them. However, the men began following her and on the corner of Brick Lane and Wentworth Street they attacked. The men punched her to the ground, kicked her face and stole her purse. One of them then lifted her skirt and rammed something into her vagina. It was this blow that would kill her for it ruptured her internal organs, causing heavy internal bleeding that could not be stopped.

The case was handed to Chief Inspector West of H Division of the Metropolitan Police, which covered the Whitechapel area. West began by talking to the beat constables who covered the area around George Street and the scene of the crime. They had neither seen nor heard anything on the night of the attack. However they did know that a couple of gangs of street toughs operated a protection racket, extorting money from the street prostitutes in return for a form of protection that amounted to little more than not being robbed by the self same gang.

There was a strong suspicion among the police that the belligerent Smith had refused to pay and had been attacked as a result. It was not normal for any gang to use such extreme violence, knowing as they did that they could easily end up on the scaffold. It was thought that perhaps the younger man singled out by Smith had been a new gang member who had overstepped the mark. With their only witness dead, and with the beat constables unable to find anyone who was willing to give evidence against the gang, the trail rapidly went cold.

The inquest was held in front of the coroner Wynne Baxter on Saturday 7 April. The murder of anyone on the streets of London was a rare event. Even if the victim was only a street prostitute from Whitechapel, the capital was agog for details and so too was the nation at large. *The Times* newspaper sent a reporter to the inquest who filed the following report, which was printed on Monday 9 April:

Mr. Wynne E. Baxter, the East Middlesex Coroner, held an inquiry on Saturday [7 Apr] at the London Hospital respecting the death of

EMMA ELIZABETH SMITH, aged 45, a widow, lately living at 18, George-street, Spitalfields, who, it was alleged, had been murdered.

Chief Inspector West, of the H Division of Police, attended for the Commissioners of Police.

Mrs. Mary Russell, deputy keeper of a common lodging-house, stated that she had known the deceased for about two years. On the evening of Bank Holiday [2 Apr] she left home at 7 o'clock, and returned about 4 or 5 the next morning in a dreadful state. Her face and head were much injured, one of her ears being nearly torn off. She told the witness that she had been set upon and robbed of all her money. She also complained of pains in the lower part of the body. Witness took her to the hospital, and when passing along Osborne-street the deceased pointed out the spot where she was assaulted. She said there were three men, but she could not describe them.

Mr. George Haslip, house surgeon, stated that when the deceased was admitted to the hospital she had been drinking but was not intoxicated. She was bleeding from the head and ear, and had other injuries of a revolting nature. Witness found that she was suffering from rupture of the peritoneum, which had been perforated by some blunt instrument used with great force. The deceased told him that at half past 1 that morning she was passing near Whitechapel Church when she noticed some men coming towards her. She crossed the road to avoid them, but they followed, assaulted her, took all the money she had, and then committed the outrage. She was unable to say what kind of instrument was used, nor could she describe her assailants, except that she said that one was a youth of 19. Death ensued on Wednesday morning [4 Apr] through peritonitis set up by the injuries.

Margaret Hayes, living at the same address as the deceased, deposed to seeing Mrs. Smith in company with a man at the corner of Farrant-street and Burdett-road. The man was dressed in a dark suit and wore a white silk handkerchief round his neck. He was of medium height, but witness did not think she could identify him.

Chief Inspector West, H Division, stated that he had no official information on the subject, and was only aware of the case through the daily papers. He had questioned the constables on the beat, but none of them appeared to know anything about the matter.

The Coroner said that from the medical evidence, which must be true, it was clear that the woman had been barbarously murdered. It was impossible to imagine a more brutal and dastardly assault, and he thought the ends of justice would be better met by the jury recording their verdict at once than by adjourning to some future date in the hope of having more evidence brought before them.

The jury returned a verdict of 'Wilful murder against some person or persons unknown'.

THE PROBLEMS OF PROSTITUTION

Reports on the case continued to appear in the more local newspapers for several days afterwards. On 15 April the *Sunday People* used the murder as a hook on which to hang a piece about the vice trade in London and the need to clear the prostitutes off the streets. It ended:

The state of our London streets at night is an old subject and a sore one. It cannot be said that at any time within memory of living man their condition has been particularly creditable to the greatest capital in the world. Still, there certainly was a time, and that not very long ago, when things were very much less disgraceful than they are now. The seamy side of London life which is revealed to anybody whose homeward way lies through Regent-

street or Piccadilly at midnight is positively shameful. Cases (one in particular our readers will remember which is not yet decided) are continually arising of riot and assault by women as well as men; and the police are powerless to prevent solicitation and annoyance. The reason is that since the 'Cass Case' the constables have orders to arrest no women for solicitation unless they are actually given in charge, a step which is not always easy or safe to take. The consequence is that it is impossible for any decent man to go quietly along without being accosted, and perhaps assaulted, by women and their male companions. This must be altered and the absurd order to the police rescinded. Otherwise there will be nothing done but to form a strong vigilance committee to obtain evidence in a sufficient number of cases to strike terror into these evil birds of the night. At present respectable people are practically at their mercy.

The Cass Case referred to concerned the arrest of an entirely respectable, if poor, woman named Elizabeth Cass. She was arrested when out shopping on the evening of 28 June 1887, thrown into prison and charged with street prostitution. The arresting policeman was convinced that Miss Cass was a woman who had escaped him three times before by running off and that this time he had finally got her. It turned out to be a case of mistaken identity. Miss Cass was eventually released amid much embarrassment all round.

By the end of April even the local East End press had lost interest in the brutal murder of Emma Smith. The lack of anything new to say and the lack of progress by the police investigation meant that other news was taking the public's attention. It would not be long before that news took a turn very much for the worse.

CHAPTER 4:

MURDER MOST HORRIBLE

I n Victorian times, the city of London was simply not accustomed to vicious, random murders, so the discovery of a dead woman whose body had been horribly mutilated came as a complete shock to everyone. As the gruesome details of the murder began to emerge, the people of London were at first horrified, then mystified, then frightened to death as it became clear the killer was still at large.

THE FIRST BODY IS FOUND

It was the *Evening Star* newspaper on 7 August 1888 that first alerted Londoners to the coming terror. Tucked away on page 3 in the section reserved for late breaking news was a short story headlined 'A Whitechapel Horror'. The story was short and to the point, but lacked many details. It ran:

> *A woman, now lying unidentified at the mortuary, Whitechapel, was ferociously stabbed to death this morning, between two and four o'clock, on the landing of a stone staircase in George's-buildings, Whitechapel.*
>
> *George's-buildings are tenements occupied by the poor labouring class. A lodger going early to his work found the body. Another lodger says the murder was not committed when he returned home about two o'clock. The woman was stabbed in 20 places. No*

weapon was found near her, and the murderer has left no trace. She is of middle age and height, has black hair and a large, round face, and apparently belonged to the lowest class.

By 9 August the *London Echo* had rather more details. The story in that newspaper ran as follows:

THE WHITECHAPEL MYSTERY.
NO TRACE OF THE MURDERER.

INQUEST ON THE VICTIM.

Although two days have passed since the body of a woman – who is not yet identified – was found in the passage of 37, George-yard-buildings, Whitechapel, the discovery is still enveloped in mystery. The officials at the Criminal Investigation Department have been actively engaged in searching for a clue which may lead to the capture of the presumed murderer, but no arrest has yet been made. The inquest was opened this afternoon by Deputy Coroner Collier, in the library of the Working Lads' Institute, Whitechapel-road. Inspectors Ellisdon and Reid watched the case on behalf of the police authorities.

DID NOT SEE THE BODY. *Elizabeth Mahoney said she lived at 47, George-yard-buildings. It was an artisans' dwellings' house, and one of the rules was that all the lights should be put out on the staircase after eleven o'clock. Witness went out on Bank Holiday and returned with her husband about two o'clock on Tuesday morning. She afterwards went down the staircase again to get something for supper. She saw no one on the staircase, and heard no noise, but she admitted that she had no light with her, and it was possible for her to pass up the staircase without being aware of the body of the woman lying there.*

SAW SOME ONE – 'TOOK NO NOTICE.' *Alfred George Crow, a cabdriver, said he lived at No. 35 in the same block of buildings. He returned home on Tuesday morning at about half-past three, and passed up the staircase in which the deceased was found. He noticed some one lying on the first landing. He took no notice of the fact, as people constantly slept on the stairs.*

HOW THE BODY WAS DISCOVERED. *John Reeves, the man who first discovered the body of the deceased, was then examined. He said he lived at No. 37, George-yard-buildings. He was a waterside labourer. On Tuesday morning he left home about five o'clock to go to work. On reaching the first landing he found the body of a female. The woman was lying in a pool of blood, on her back. He did not examine her further. He was frightened, and gave information to the police.*

A SOON-TO-BE-FAMILIAR MODUS OPERANDI

Those few paragraphs covered a mass of activity by the police. It was at a few minutes before 5 am when PC Thomas Barrett's regular beat patrol was interrupted by a man, John Reeves, who was shouting that he had found a dead body. Barrett followed Reeves to George Yard Buildings in

Wentworth Street and followed him up the stairs to the first floor where he found a dead woman. The body had been arranged in a gross parody of a woman having sex, her legs akimbo and facing toward the stairs leading up to the second floor. The woman's skirts had been pushed up to reveal her naked groin, which had been stabbed numerous times. A huge pool of blood covered much of the landing. Barrett sent Reeves off to summon a doctor and more policemen while he guarded the body and crime scene.

Detectives were on the scene quickly. By 5.30 am the area had been searched for clues, but none were found. The body was then taken to Dr Timothy Killeen for an autopsy, which took place later that day. Dr Killeen reported that the woman had been murdered at about 2.30 am, the cause of death being blood loss from the stab wounds. There were 39 wounds in all, most of them inflicted to the breasts, belly and groin. Killeen believed that 38 of the wounds had been inflicted by an ordinary clasp knife, but that one was much deeper and narrower than such a knife could inflict.

The woman herself was fairly plump, middle aged and seemed to be in good health. She had been wearing a black bonnet, long black jacket, dark green skirt, brown petticoat, stockings and spring-sided boots. Although the clothes were all reasonably clean and well kept, they were of poor quality and all showed signs of age, especially the boots which were heavily worn. Clearly the dead woman was fairly poor, even by Whitechapel standards.

The location of the murder must have struck most people as being a bit odd. George Yard was rather misleadingly named as it was more an alley than a yard. It ran from Wentworth Street south to Whitechapel High Street. The entrances at both ends were narrow, barely wide enough for a horse and cart to gain access, but it was wider along its length. At the High Street end, the yard passed under a low brick arch and the courtyard of a pub, the White Hart. George Yard Buildings occupied the west side of this alley at its northern end, closest to Wentworth Street.

The Buildings took the form of a brick-built tenement three storeys tall. There was only one access, a brick Gothic-style arch that led to a hallway and the staircase. The buildings had a live-in manager who occupied a small apartment on the first floor and had an office next to the entrance. The manager went off duty at 10 pm and routinely went around switching off the gaslights that illuminated the corridors and stairs. There were over 45 separate rooms and apartments of various sizes within the buildings, each occupied by at least one tenant. The entrance itself was always open and never locked, for the simple reason that several of those who rented accommodation there worked shifts and needed to get in and out at all hours of the day and night.

As with the open areas of other residential properties, the stairs and corridors of George Yard Buildings made for a tempting resting place for those too poor, or too drunk, to gain admittance to even a common lodging house. Nor was it unknown for street prostitutes to take their clients to such a place to conduct their business out of the cold or the rain. But as a place to conduct a murder it seemed utterly outlandish. Residents went in and out all the time, so a murderer could expect to be interrupted at any time. And if the person interrupting was a burly factory worker he might well decide to attack the killer, the first step in taking the murderer to the gallows.

THE POLICE GO INTO ACTION

Right from the start, the murder was odd to the point of being bizarre. Nevertheless, the police went into action. They began by knocking on all the doors in George Yard, and in Wentworth Street and Whitechapel High Street. The detectives wanted to know if anyone had heard or seen anything untoward at around 2.30 am, and in particular if anyone knew the dead woman. In this last quest they were helped by a new development in technology: photography. A photograph was taken of the dead woman's face and shoulders before the post-mortem began. Dozens of copies of the photo were printed off and given to the policemen conducting door-to-door inquiries in the hope that somebody would recognize the woman.

The case was given to Inspector Edmund Reid. Reid had come late to the police force, having previously earned his living as a cook both in London and on board merchant ships. He joined the Met in 1872 at the age of 26 as a regular beat constable. Two years later he moved to the CID and in 1880 was promoted to be Detective Sergeant. By 1888 he was the head of the CID in H Division, which covered Whitechapel, and was therefore the most senior detective in the area. The police could not be accused of taking the murder lightly. Reid also had a career outside the police. He was an amateur balloonist, going up in hot air balloons at least 23 times – and in 1877 had made Britain's first descent from a balloon by parachute. He was also a gifted amateur actor and singer of operettas.

The first witness to produce some potentially useful information was PC Barrett himself. At 2 am he had been patrolling down Wentworth Street when he spotted a man loitering. When Barrett saw the man was wearing an army uniform he thought of the Grenadier Guards, and went over for a chat. After remarking on the weather, Barrett suggested it was a bit late and about time the soldier should be getting back to barracks. The soldier replied that he would be off shortly and that he was 'waiting for a chum who has gone off with a girl'. Barrett passed on. Now the incident assumed new importance. It had been only half an hour before the estimated time of death and the deep, narrow wound might have been caused by a bayonet. Barrett's superiors set about arranging an identity parade.

Meanwhile the residents of George Yard Buildings had been telling their stories. Joseph and Elizabeth Mahoney lived on the top floor. Elizabeth Mahoney's statement ran as follows:

Monday was Bank Holiday, and my husband and I were out all day, and did not return until twenty minutes to two on Tuesday morning. We went straight up to our room, and after taking off my hat and cloak, I came down again and went to a chandler's shop in Thrawl-street to buy some provisions for supper. I came back having been gone about five minutes; and after having supper we went to bed. On neither occasion, either in coming up or going down the stairs, did I see the body of a woman lying there. It is quite possible that a body might have been there, and that I did not notice it, because the stairs are very wide and were completely dark, all the lights having, as usual, been turned out at eleven o'clock. I did not get up till half-past eight in the morning, and during the night my attention was not attracted by a noise or disturbance of any kind.

The first the Mahoneys knew of the murder was when the police knocked loudly on their door.

Alfred Crow lived on the first floor. He had come home after a night out at 3.30 am. He too said it was very dark on the stairs, but he had clearly seen the body. He had taken it for a vagrant sleeping on the landing, and had left it alone. He too was first alerted to the murder by the police.

Of key importance were Francis and Amy Hewitt who lived on the first floor and outside whose door the woman had been killed. Not only that, but Francis Hewitt was the manager of the buildings, responsible for their upkeep and the collecting of rent.

Mrs Hewitt proved to be a reluctant witness, merely saying that she agreed with what her husband said. Francis was a painter and decorator. He said that he and his wife had been in all evening. Early the previous evening they had heard a disturbance outside, but had heard nothing from inside the building at about 2.30 am as they had been asleep. Given that the distance from the body to their bed was barely 12 feet, with only a wooden door between them, the police quickly concluded that the killer had been remarkably quick and quiet.

THE ROLE OF THE PRESS

Hewitt later told a newspaper reporter that he thought the woman had been murdered by a man after they came up the stairs and had an argument. Whether this was because he had actually heard something or if he was merely guessing in order to please the reporter was never clear.

The police knew that the vast majority of murders were committed by a relative or acquaintance of the victim. The pattern of stab wounds to the body indicated an interest in the sex organs, which in turn pointed to a sexual motive. Perhaps the killer was a husband or lover to whom the woman had been unfaithful, or perhaps the killer had been a man spurned by the victim. With nothing much in the way of evidence coming from the scene of the crime, the police were desperate to identify the woman. Newspapers printed engravings based on the mortuary photo in the hope this would lead to an identification.

At this date there was no formal relationship between the police and the press. Police inspectors did not hold press conferences at which they shared news with the reporters, nor did they issue appeals for witnesses through the press. Nevertheless, neither the police nor the press were ignorant of the uses of the other. Reporters would talk to police constables and detectives working on a case in the hope of getting information, just as they routinely spoke to witnesses, victims and their relatives. The police also knew that the press could reach a wider public more quickly than they could hope to do themselves. Detectives would often remark to reporters that they were seeking such and such a person, or wanted to question a person matching a particular description. Police were also keenly aware that the media existed to sell newspapers and might be inclined to sensationalize a case. As a result, senior police were often wary about speaking to reporters and would withhold information if they thought it might be better if the public were not aware of certain facts.

In this case, the police did not share with the reporters details of the horrible wounds inflicted on the dead woman. They said merely that there were numerous stab wounds. Rumour and gossip, however, went rapidly into overdrive. It was very quickly clear from the way the police were acting that this murder was something special. That the victim had been 'cut up', 'butchered' or 'horribly mutilated' was within hours being spoken of in pubs and on the streets. Murders in Whitechapel were rare, brutal killings involving mutilations were unheard of.

THE FIRST OF MANY DEAD ENDS

Meanwhile the best lead was the idling soldier, so Reid pursued that line of inquiry. On 8 August Barrett had been taken to the Tower of London where the Grenadier Guards were based. Barrett had described the soldier as being '22–26 years of age, 5 feet 9 or 10 inches tall, fair complexioned with a small brown moustache turned up at the ends. He had no medals, but wore one good conduct badge on his tunic'. Also taking part in the parade was a Mrs Goldhawk of Aldgate who had seen a woman matching the dead woman's description with a soldier on the night of the murder.

The men were paraded while Barrett and Mrs Goldhawk walked up and down the lines. Goldhawk did not recognize anyone, but Barrett picked out two who he said looked like the man he had met, though he could not be absolutely certain. One of the soldiers was at once ruled out since he had been in barracks, but the other – Private John Leary – had been out for the night in question. When interviewed Leary said he and Private Law had gone out drinking in the City until the pubs closed, after which they had gone for a walk up The Strand and Charing Cross, returning later to Billingsgate where the market pubs were open in the early morning and heading back to barracks at 6 am. Law confirmed the story.

Another guardsman, Private Benjamin, had gone absent without leave on the Sunday. When he finally showed up back at the Tower of London he was at once arrested, his clothing and possessions impounded and word sent to Reid. When the inspector arrived, Benjamin said that he had rushed off to visit his family in Kingston upon Thames due to a sudden family crisis. He had not been due to be on duty and so had not bothered to tell his officer that he was leaving. Reid took a detailed statement about Benjamin's movements, then despatched a policeman to check them out. Everything tallied. Benjamin had been seen by several people in Kingston on the night of the murder and was ruled out.

MARTHA TABRAM IS IDENTIFIED

On the morning of 10 August two people came forward to say they recognized the dead woman. Unfortunately they gave two different names, so the police had to do further digging before they could be sure which was correct. One man, James Hunt, was a resident of Guildford, Surrey. His wife had left him some years earlier to seek a better life in London. Having read about the murder and the description of the victim he thought it might be his wife. The other possible identity was that of Emma Turner, a prostitute living at Satchell's Lodging House,

19 George Street in Spitalfields, who had not been seen since the night of the murder. Reid thought Turner the more likely victim, so police began their inquiries accordingly. On 15 August a Mary Connelly firmly identified the corpse as that of Emma Turner.

Connelly was also a prostitute who worked the streets of the East End. She said that she and Emma had often worked together, and had done so on the night of the murder. They had met a soldier and a corporal, both of the Scots Guards, at about 10 pm in the Two Brewers on Brick Lane. The four had continued drinking and chatting, moving on to other pubs, for some time. By midnight they were in Wentworth Street and the soldiers made it clear that it was time for sex.

Connelly took her corporal into a narrow alley while Emma led her client into George Yard. When Connelly had finished and been paid she and her corporal returned to Wentworth Road. She then left him waiting for his friend.

The story tallied with what Reid knew so far. PC Barrett had seen a soldier waiting in Wentworth Street for a friend who had gone off with a girl. Now Connelly had seen the victim go off with a soldier to George Yard, where her body was later found. Presumably the corporal left by Connelly was the same soldier seen by Barrett – though they had identified them as belonging to different regiments. The times did not quite match. Connelly said she left her soldier at about 12.30 while Barrett met his around 2 am – and the time of death was about 3 am – but they were fairly close.

Although it was looking likely that the killer was a soldier, Reid, now he had a name for the victim, could investigate her movements, friends and relatives. Emma Turner had been for some years living with a carpenter named Henry Turner as his wife. In fact the two were not married for the simple reason that 'Emma Turner' was already married. Turner revealed that her real name had been Martha Tabram. She had been born Martha White in London in 1849, making her 39 years old at the time of her murder. Her father had died in 1865 and in 1869 she married Henry Tabram of Newington after the couple had already been living together for some weeks. Tabram was a foreman on a good wage, so the young couple could afford their own house and smart clothes. In 1871 a son, Frederick, was born and the following year a second son, Charles. But before long things began to go wrong. Martha took to drink, though why was not recorded. By 1875 Tabram was so worried by Martha's influence on the boys and her drinking that he kicked her out of the house, arranging to pay her 12 shillings a week maintenance. This was a sizeable sum and would have been enough to keep Martha in some comfort. But her drinking put paid to that. She spent every penny she had on drink, allowing her clothing and personal hygiene to suffer, and began living in common lodging houses.

When Tabram heard his estranged wife had found a new man, he stopped paying her any maintenance at all. Martha continued drinking, though at first Turner does not seem to have minded. She would often go off on drinking binges that could last all night, though at other times she did her duties as a housewife well enough. Not that Turner was fussy. Those who knew him described him as being dirty, slovenly and badly dressed.

By the spring of 1888 Turner was out of work. Instead of earning a living by carpentry he was walking the streets selling pins, needles and other trinkets from a tray. The couple were renting a room from Mrs Mary Bousfield at 4 Star Place, Commercial Road. Reid tracked down Bousfield and questioned her about Martha and Turner. Bousfield said that Martha had always preferred a glass of beer to a cup of tea and was sometimes very drunk, though as a rule she was merely tipsy much of the time. Bousfield also suspected that Martha was earning money as a street prostitute, though she also sold matches on street corners.

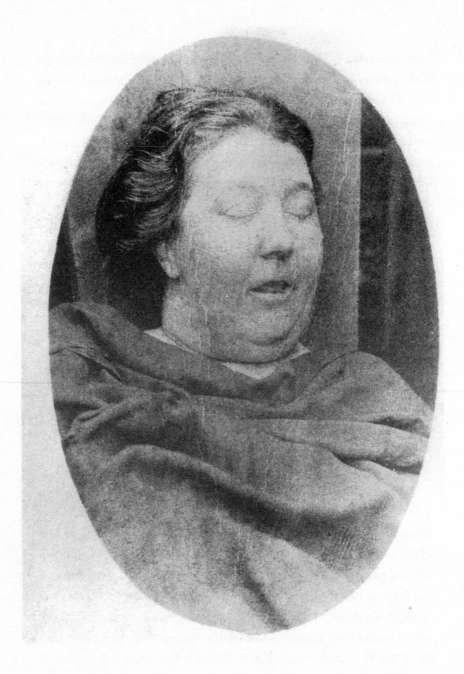

The mortuary photograph of Martha Tabram. Photography was then in its infancy and was seen as a vital modern aid in the fight against crime.

At the end of June Martha and Turner had left their lodgings, owing a sizeable amount in back rent. Bousfield had not seen them since, though Martha had come back a few days later and left the money for the unpaid rent with a note.

When Turner was tracked down, Reid questioned him about what he and Martha had been doing since they left Commercial Road. He said that he had split from Martha, having become exasperated at her heavy drinking and by the way that she spent any money he gave her on drink rather than what it had been intended for. He said that he had not seen her for some weeks, but had then bumped into her on 4 August in Leadenhall Street in the City of London. She was, he said, destitute and penniless. Taking pity on her he had given her trinkets from his tray worth one shilling and sixpence in the hope that she would sell them to make money. He advised her to spend any money she raised on new stock to make further profits, but suspected it would just go on drink. He had, he said, never seen her again. Turner's account of his movements checked out, so he was written off as a suspect.

A MURDER WITHOUT A MOTIVE – OR A SUSPECT

That left Reid with a victim who had been a heavy-drinking woman working as a street prostitute, apparently for some months, who had last been seen with a soldier and who had, moreover, suffered a wound that looked very much as if it had been caused by a bayonet. PC Barrett had seen a soldier near the scene of the crime, while prostitute Mary Ann Connelly had spent some hours with the victim and her soldier client. It was time to identify the soldiers.

Unfortunately Connelly had vanished. The police were both annoyed at having lost a witness and concerned in case the killer had come back to silence her. After a good deal of investigation, Connelly was found staying with a cousin in Drury Lane and hauled back to Whitechapel for further questioning. Connelly had said that the soldiers were from the Scots Guards, not the Grenadier Guards, so a new identity parade was arranged for her. Sergeant Caunter of the Whitechapel CID led her around the serried ranks of the Scots Guards, but barely had they begun when Connelly declared that the two men she had met were not there. When asked how she could be sure, she replied that the men she had met had had white bands on their hats, something the Scots Guards did not have.

A hurried discussion between Caunter and the officers of the Scots Guards revealed that only one regiment with men based in London had white bands on their hats: the Coldstream Guards. Another identity parade was arranged with the Coldstreamers at their barracks on 15 August.

This time Connelly picked out two men she said she recognized: Privates Skipper and George. Although neither was a corporal, they did both have good conduct badges as seen by both Connelly and Barrett. It soon transpired that both men had been quietly tucked up in bed on the night of the murder and had numerous witnesses to prove it. Another lead had gone cold.

On 19 August Reid finally tracked down Henry Tabram. Any lingering thoughts that the murder may have been committed by the estranged husband for some reason were quickly laid to rest. Tabram lived in Greenwich and worked on the ships plying the North Sea. He had been out of the country when the murder took place.

The coroner's inquest resumed and was completed on 23 August. Deputy Coroner George Collier heard the key elements of the evidence again, with Connelly, Turner and Bousfield giving evidence in person. In his summing-up Collier said that 'the crime was one of the most brutal that has occurred for some years. For a poor defenceless woman to be outraged and stabbed in the manner in which this woman has been is almost beyond belief.' The jury returned a verdict of wilful murder by some person or persons unknown.

That the crime had attracted more than the usual interest is shown by the fact that as well as being reported in the London and national newspapers, the inquest rated a mention in the *Bradford Observer* in Yorkshire. The *Manchester Guardian* also carried a lengthy article.

Reid drew up a report on the case so far and took it to Donald Swanson, Chief Inspector of CID at Scotland Yard. This was a routine move in any crime that remained unsolved and appeared to be unlikely to be solved. Swanson went over the file and arranged for witnesses to be asked additional questions. From Dr Killeen he obtained the important clarification that the deep, narrow wound had been made by a narrow, flat-bladed knife and not by a bayonet, which was triangular in cross section. Killeen was of the opinion that two different knives had been used – one to kill and then a second to stab the body repeatedly.

RIGHT-HANDED MAN

The wounds had all been caused by a right-handed man and had apparently been inflicted quickly and rapidly, with only vague efforts at aiming the blows. It was as if the attack had taken place in great anger or emotional stress. One wound, however, was different. That wound was about three inches long and one inch deep and ran down towards the groin. Unlike the other wounds it was a cut, not a stab, and it appeared to have been made quite deliberately.

Swanson was also of the opinion that Connelly and Barrett were now discredited as witnesses when it came to identifying a suspect. They had both positively identified as the mystery soldier men who had proved to have cast iron alibis. Even if one of them now identified a man who did not have an alibi the identification would be useless in court.

Chief Inspector Donald Swanson, pictured after he retired in 1903.

Swanson also went over the times given by the different witnesses and clarified those. It was clear that the murder had taken place after 1.50 am when the Mahoneys had climbed the stairs and before 3.30 am when Alfred Crow saw the body, but thought it was someone sleeping. It was equally clear that Martha had serviced her client at around midnight. Even though Connelly had not waited for her, it was impossible to believe that the act had taken place beyond 12.30 am. Although PC Barrett had said he saw the soldier at 2 am, he had not noted it in his notebook so it was possible the incident had occurred when he had walked down the street at 1 am. All in all, Swanson concluded that Martha Tabram had finished with her soldiers by 12.30 or 1 am at the very latest. She had then probably found another client and taken him also to the stairwell in George's Yard. This new client had then murdered her.

Reid was confident that he had tracked down and eliminated everyone who had known Martha Tabram. The killing had not been carried out for any personal reason to do with Tabram and seemed to have been committed by someone who had not previously known the victim. And yet the nature of the injuries and wounds indicated the killer had acted in anger or frenzy. That was unlikely if the killing had been the result of a dispute over, say, the price charged by Tabram for her services. There was no possible motive for the murder. The assault on Smith at least had some likely cause, but in the Tabram case there was nothing. Nevertheless there were now two dead women in Whitechapel, both prostitutes and both having suffered horrific injuries to the groin area. The police were left with the uncomfortable option that some sort of lunatic was at large.

It was now almost two weeks after the murder had taken place. Every lead the police had found had petered out without finding a suspect.

On the streets, however, the murder was not forgotten. On 25 August Francis Hewitt wrote a short but angry letter to the editor of the *Sunday People* about a report in that newspaper that had been causing him difficulties. It read:

Sir, – My attention has been drawn to a report in your issue of the 12th inst. Under the above heading. In it the following statements occur:– (1) That a number of the tenants of George Yard Buildings 'let beds by the night to travellers.' (2) That consequently, 'men go there with women, whom they represent to be their wives.' On behalf of the tenants, I beg to give these statements an unqualified denial. Beds are let by the night in this locality, but never in these buildings.

Hewitt was suffering other problems. As reported in a small article in the *East London Observer* he was plagued by a constant stream of visitors to the buildings that he cared for.

There have been many visitors to George-yard-buildings since the murder with the rather morbid purpose of seeing the place where the deceased was discovered. Here there is still a large surface of the stone flags crimson-stained. It is at the spot where the blood oozed from the poor creature's heart.

Interest in the bizarre, horrifying and deeply disturbing murder of Martha Tabram was hardly fading by the end of August. That nobody had been caught merely added to the air of mystery and terror that surrounded the killing. Nobody knew why Tabram had been singled out for slaughter. Women, and particularly prostitutes, wondered if they might be next. But life had to go on. Those women too destitute to do anything other than rely on prostitution had to work the streets or starve.

By 30 August daily life in Whitechapel had gone back to normal. That was about to change.

CHAPTER 5:

THE TERROR BEGINS

It was the second murder in less than a month in London's East End that tipped London into a frenzy of fear and recrimination. Rumours were rife everywhere you went, people spoke about little else and the authorities suddenly came under massive pressure to do something about the situation. Two women had now been murdered and mutilated, apparently at random. Nobody was safe on the streets and women walked in fear. What were they going to do about it?

MURDER NUMBER TWO

At 3.45 am on the morning of 31 August PC John Neil was walking with the officially approved steady, measured tread along Buck's Row, a street that ran parallel to Whitechapel Road, a few yards north of the main road. The street was cobbled, wide enough for carts to pass and flanked on each side by pavements. It was lined by small cottages and workshops but was not well lit, having only one street lamp.

As Neil walked along he noticed something lying on the north side pavement close to a gateway leading to a stable yard. It was dark, so he shone his torch at the object and found it was a woman lying on her back, eyes staring up to the sky and bonnet lying a few feet away. Her legs were pushed up and apart in the same grim parody of sex that had been the case with the body of Martha Tabram.

Neil then heard footsteps in Brady Street at the end of Buck's Row and when another policeman appeared, PC John Thain, Neil called him over. Together the two men inspected the woman, finding that her neck had been savagely cut open, but that the body was still warm. Using their lamps they looked around the area for any possible clues but found nothing. A nearby patch of mud showed no footprints or wheel marks.

Thain had patrolled down Buck's Row just half an hour earlier and had not seen anything then. Neil sent Thain off to rouse Dr Rees Ralph Llewellyn who lived nearby. As Thain left a third policeman came running up. This was Jonas Mizen, who had been walking down Hanbury Street when two men had come up to him to report finding a woman either drunk or injured lying in Buck's Row. After taking the men's names,

PC John Neil discovers the mutilated body of the second victim in Buck's Row, just outside the closed gates of a stable yard.

Charles Cross and Robert Paul, Mizen had set off to see if he could help the woman. Mizen brought the news that the two men had found the woman with her skirt lifted up to reveal her groin and stomach, but had pulled the skirt down for the sake of decency before setting off to find a patrolling policeman. Mizen was sent off to find an ambulance to take the body to the mortuary.

By this time three men walking home from working the late shift at a nearby company had seen the police and come over to see what was happening. The resulting conversation woke up the residents of the cottages, who also looked or came out to see what was happening. Neil was keeping the growing crowd away from the body and the surrounding crime scene. Eventually Dr Llewellyn arrived to confirm what the policemen already knew, that the woman was dead. The body was taken off to the mortuary to be studied next morning. Thain was then sent off to the police station to find an inspector – it was Inspector Joseph Helson who was on duty – and alert him to the finding of another murder victim in Whitechapel.

GRUESOME MUTILATIONS

As with the finding of the body that turned out to be Martha Tabram, the police began by knocking on doors along Buck's Row and neighbouring roads to see if anyone had seen or heard anything odd between 3.15 am when PC Thain had patrolled down Buck's Row and 3.45 am when the body was found. Again, the police had a photo of the dead woman taken at the mortuary in the hope that somebody would recognize her.

There had been nothing on the body to identify her. Before Dr Llewellyn had carried out the autopsy, two mortuary employees, Robert Mann and James Hatfield, had emptied the woman's pockets and guarded the body until Inspector John Spratling arrived and the autopsy began. Her only possessions were a comb, a white pocket handkerchief and a small broken piece of mirror. The clothes were mostly of poor quality, old and in places stained but generally clean and in good condition. The dress was, however, fairly new and better quality than the rest. One of the two petticoats the woman had been wearing was stamped 'Lambeth Workhouse'. As soon as this was reported to Inspector Helson he sent a constable armed with a photo of the dead woman to the workhouse to try to get an identification.

Llewellyn and Spratling formed the opinion that the dead woman was very poor, almost destitute and guessed that she might have earned a living as a prostitute.

Dr Llewellyn then moved on to the autopsy proper and made some very gruesome finds. His later report ran:

Five teeth were missing, and there was a slight laceration of the tongue. There was a bruise running along the lower part of the jaw on the right side of the face. That might have been caused by a blow from a fist or pressure from a thumb. There was a circular bruise on the left side of the face which also might have been inflicted by the pressure of the fingers. On the left side of the neck, about 1 in. below the jaw, there was an incision about 4 in. in length, and ran from a point immediately below the ear. On the same side, but an inch below, and commencing about 1 in. in front of it, was a circular incision, which terminated at a point about 3 in. below the right jaw. That incision completely severed all the tissues down to the vertebrae. The large vessels of the neck on both sides were severed. The incision was about 8 in. in length. The cuts must have been caused by a long-bladed knife, moderately sharp, and used with great violence. No blood was found on the breast, either of the body or the clothes. There were no injuries about the body until just about the lower part of the abdomen. Two or three inches from the left side was a wound running in a jagged manner. The wound was a very deep one, and the tissues were cut through. There were several incisions running across the abdomen. There were three or four similar cuts running downwards, on the right side, all of which had been caused by a knife which had been used violently and downwards. The injuries were from left to right and might have been done by a left handed person. All the injuries had been caused by the same instrument.

TERRIBLE DEATH

The dead woman had first been punched or gripped by the jaw, and then had her throat cut so completely that she bled to death within seconds. The skirt and petticoats had then been lifted up and the series of cuts and slashes made to the abdomen and the groin area. The nature of the mutilations was not made fully public by the police. This was partly out of a sense of decency and regard for the dead woman and whoever her relatives might turn out to be, but also because the police did not want all and sundry to be aware of exactly what had taken place. They wanted it kept between them and the killer.

Back on the street, the police door-to-door questioning was proving to be fruitless. Among the first to be questioned were the Green family, who lived in the cottage outside which the body had been found. The head of the family was Emma Green, who lived there with her two adult sons and a daughter, her husband having died some years earlier. She reported that her two sons had gone to bed before 10 pm, sleeping in the back room. She and her daughter had gone to bed in the upstairs front room at 11 pm and had slept through until 4 am when the noise of the policemen talking outside had woken them up. Mrs Green declared herself to be a fairly light sleeper. Since her bed was barely 20 feet from the body and separated from it by only an ill-fitting window, this meant that the killing and mutilations must have been carried out in near silence, as had been the case with the killing of Martha Tabram.

A vigilant named Patrick Mulshaw had been on night duty in Winthrop Street, a side street off Buck's Row. He was employed by the Board of Works and was guarding a hole in the road where a sewer was being repaired, along with the workmen's tools that were left on site. He stated that he had been wide awake, sitting on his chair between 3 am and 4 am. He had earlier seen PC Neil on patrol. Like Mrs Green he had heard nothing, nor had he seen the victim enter Buck's Row nor a man leaving it.

Given where Mulshaw had been sitting, this almost certainly meant that the victim and her killer had entered Buck's Row from the west end, from Baker's Row (now Vallance Road), and that the killer had left again by the same route. Walter and Mary Purkiss and their family had also been close by. Purkiss was the manager of the Essex Wharf workshop on the south side of the street some 20 yards from where the murder had taken place. He lived on site with his family, he and his wife sharing a room that looked out on to the street. Mary Purkiss was not very well that night and had woken up at a little after 3 am. She had got out of bed and paced about the room for half an hour before going back to bed and falling asleep. Like Mrs Green she had heard no noises from the street.

Inspector Spratling was by mid morning back on Buck's Row having witnessed the autopsy and was by now fully aware of how serious the crime was. Assisted by Sergeant George Godley, Spratling called again at all of the nearby properties, but discovered nothing new. He ordered a thorough search to be made of all yards, gutters and pavements in the area as well as the railway lines of the District Railway that lay just south of Buck's Row.

The railway workers were questioned, and one of them came up with something that sounded positive. Signalman Thomas Ede said that he had seen a man acting suspiciously in Darling Row, about 300 yards east of the murder scene. He said the man had been furtive and odd. Ede described the man as being slender, walking with a slight limp, standing 5ft 8in in height, 35 years of age with a dark moustache and whiskers. He had been wearing a double peaked cap, dark brown jacket and a pair of clean overalls and dark trousers. It was not much to go on, but at least it was something.

NEWS OF THE MURDERS SPREADS

The evening after the body had been found the *Evening Echo* carried a story under the headline 'HORRIBLE MURDER IN WHITECHAPEL'. Given how soon after the body had been discovered the story was written and printed it was remarkably full and accurate. It also gives a fairly accurate picture of what the police thought about the crime at this early date.

A tragedy, even more revolting in its details than that of George-yard, and surrounded apparently with circumstances fully as mysterious, has just occurred at Bucks-row, a low class neighbourhood, adjoining Whitechapel-road. Passing the Essex Wharf, in Bucks-row, at about 4.30 this morning, Constable Neale [sic Neil], 97J, found lying on the pavement there the dead body of a woman. On further examination her head was found to have been very nearly severed from her body. A horrible gash, fully an inch in width, extending from one side of the neck to the other, completely severing the windpipe. The lower portion of the abdomen also was completely ripped open, causing the bowels to protrude. The woman was at once conveyed to the mortuary, where she now lies. She is apparently about five and thirty years of age, with dark hair, of medium height, and with small features. Her clothing, which was examined by Inspector Nelson [sic Helson], is scanty, consisting only of a threadbare cloak with a hood, a brown dress, and a petticoat, which bears the mark of Lambeth workhouse. The woman has not yet been identified.

It is thought that the woman was assailed by some man with whom she had been in company. Her front teeth had been knocked out, the woman probably having received a kick in the mouth from her assailant.

LATER ACCOUNT. *No more revolting crime has ever been committed in Whitechapel than that which occurred in Bucks-row, Thomas-street, a comparatively unfrequented thoroughfare – especially at night – lying at the back of the Whitechapel-road. As Police-constable Neal [Neil] was leaving his beat in that locality, he saw what he first thought was a drunken woman. A closer investigation made the officer arrive at a different conclusion, for, upon stooping down, he observed that the woman's throat was literally cut from ear to ear, and her head nearly severed. The wounds in the neck extended to the spinal column. Dr. Llewelyn, of the Bethnal-green-road, was at once called. He could only pronounce it as a case of murder. It is presumed that death took place about two o'clock, for the discovery was not made until shortly before four, and the body was then warm.*

THE TERRIBLE WOUNDS. *Inspector Helston [sic Helson], Detective-Sergeant Enwright [sic Enright], and Sergeant*

Godley were soon on the spot, and made a diligent search for any weapon which might have been used in the perpetration of the crime. Their efforts in that respect were futile, but, from the nature of the injuries, it is conjectured that a knife such as would be used by butchers was wielded in the murderer's hand.

When the body of the unfortunate creature – not yet identified – was taken to the mortuary, a more minute examination showed that the actual wounds were of a character too horrible to mention in detail. As a Criminal Investigation officer remarked this afternoon, 'The injuries were such that they could only have been inflicted by a madman.'

SEARCHING FOR IDENTIFICATION. *When the body was searched, a comb and a piece of soap were found in one of the woman's pockets, and the only clue as to her previous place of abode was found on her garments, one of which showed that she had, at some time or other, been a workhouse inmate. Her life, it is thought, had been that of an immoral woman.*

NOTHING UNUSUAL HEARD. *The deceased was lying just inside the gateway of the Essex Wharf – at the corner of Bucks-row, where there is a night watchman, who, it is said, heard nothing unusual occurring in the neighbourhood last night. It is thought not improbable that the woman was murdered some little distance off, and that her body was then taken to Bucks-row and thrown inside the gateway.*

POLICE RESEARCHES. *Not only the police officers immediately engaged in the case, but the whole of the available detective force in the East-end are making a search for the slightest possible clue to the tragedy, and their investigations are materially aided by the advice of Inspector Reid, whose latest experience in crime of the kind was the dreadful affair at George-yard-buildings, when Martha Turner died from injuries, some of which are very similar in character to those inflicted upon the unknown woman found in Bucks-row. It is surmised by the detective authorities that several of the undiscovered crimes of a hideous character have been inflicted by one person, whom they think is a madman. Another theory advanced is that the deceased was mistaken for another woman, and was murdered from motives of jealousy. A feature incomprehensible to the medical man and the police engaged in the case, and one only to be accounted for by classing her murderer as a maniac, is the fact that the wounds in the woman's throat were alone sufficient to cause death. Yet there were various injuries to her body, which could only have been perpetrated for purposes of mutilation. It is this which makes the police think that the deceased was the victim of a criminal who has, while suffering from some special form of madness, wandered about London and committed crime of a mysterious nature. There is yet another suggestion, that these murders may have been the work of a gang of scoundrels who seek to levy blackmail upon unfortunate women. But it is hardly possible to believe them to have been the work of sane, however depraved people.*

THE VICTIM'S DRESS. *The deceased was dressed in a brown ulster, with metal buttons, having upon them the figure of a woman on horseback, and a man standing at the side. She had lost one tooth, but there is no appearance of any struggle, the clothes not being torn in any way. This adds to the mystery, but it is extraordinary how such wounds could have been inflicted without considerable struggling. The police, who are making the most careful investigation into the matter, express an opinion that the deceased was killed by a left-handed person, judging from the nature of the injuries. Naturally, the occurrence has caused great excitement in the crowded district in which it happened, and the scene of the tragedy was surrounded this morning by a large crowd.*

BODY IDENTIFIED AS MARY ANN NICHOLS

Meanwhile, the identity of the dead woman was being tracked down by the police. If nobody near the scene of the crime recognized her, the trip to Lambeth Workhouse had been more fruitful. Mary Ann Monk, who lived at the workhouse, recognized the photo instantly. She said the woman was a former resident named Mary Ann Nichols, who was often called Polly. Monk was taken to the mortuary to see the body and identified it at 7.30 pm on the evening of 31 August.

The following day the news of the murder had spread outside the East End of London.

The *Daily Telegraph*, which had the largest circulation in Britain, put the story on page 4 declaring, 'Another most horrible murder was perpetrated in Whitechapel yesterday morning.'

The *Daily News*, another national daily, carried extensive coverage on the front page under the headline 'BRUTAL MURDER IN WHITECHAPEL'.

The *East London Advertiser* also led with the murder, its front page declaring, 'ANOTHER WHITECHAPEL MYSTERY – HORRIBLE MURDER IN BUCK'S ROW, WHITECHAPEL'.

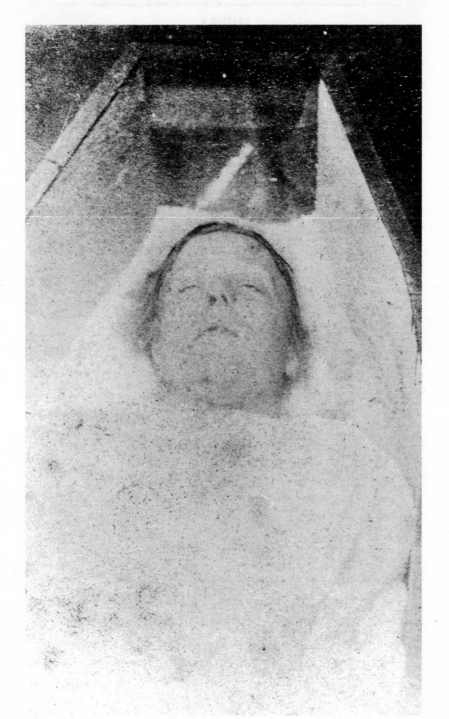

The mortuary photo of Mary Ann Nichols was instrumental in identifying the body when it was shown to residents of Lambeth Workhouse.

The *London Evening Standard* ran the headline 'MURDER IN WHITECHAPEL' and continued: 'A woman of the class known as "unfortunate" was murdered under circumstances of a most revolting character in Buck's row, Whitechapel road, yesterday morning.'

Even the upmarket *Times*, few of whose readers would ever dream of going to Whitechapel, covered the story in some detail under the headline 'ANOTHER MURDER IN WHITECHAPEL'.

Just as people had crowded to George Yard Buildings to see where Martha Tabram had died, so they flocked to Buck's Row to see where Mary Ann Nichols had perished. They found a very ordinary street, but they did not find any bloodstains. Mrs Green had got her sons to scrub the pavement and gutter clean. Although there must have been a horrible suspicion that the same person who had killed Tabram had also murdered Nichols, the police had to study the life of Nichols to see if there was any likely murder suspect, or perhaps a link to Tabram.

It took the police some days to piece together the life and habits of the murdered woman. Mary Ann 'Polly' Nichols (née Walker) had been born just off Fleet Street, London, in August 1845, making her 43 at the time of her death. Her father Edward was a blacksmith, his wife Caroline did not work. At the age of 22 she married William Nichols, who worked at the printers Perkins, Bacon & Co. The couple had five children – Edward born in 1866, Percy in 1868, Alice in 1870, Eliza in 1877 and Henry Alfred in 1879.

The marriage was not, however, a blissfully happy one. Mary Ann left on several occasions for a few days, presumably after arguments, but always went back to her husband. In 1881 she walked out for good, leaving the children with their father. The true cause of the split was never really made clear. Mary Ann's father said William had been having an affair, William maintained it was due to Mary Ann's drinking and absences. Whatever the cause, William looked after the children and paid the absent Mary Ann a weekly sum for maintenance. Soon afterwards the eldest son went to live with his grandfather.

In 1882 William discovered that Mary Ann had moved in with a new man, Thomas Dew. He stopped paying maintenance, at which point Mary Ann appealed to the parish authorities who hauled William up in front of the magistrate to get the money. William defended himself both on the grounds that he was the one looking after the children and that his wife was of depraved morals since she was working as a prostitute. He managed to prove both counts, and thereafter he and the children left Mary Ann's life.

Over the following years Mary Ann drifted from workhouse to common lodging house and back again. She was earning money as a street prostitute and in the spring of 1883 had a blazing row with her father about her lifestyle. She did not see her family again until the funeral of her brother in 1887, when she was said to be well dressed, but she largely ignored everyone.

In April 1888 she was admitted to the Lambeth Workhouse where she met the Mary Monk who would later identify her body. She proved to be a stable resident and an industrious worker, so the workhouse authorities included her in their employment programme and before long she had secured a job as a live-in maid with Mr and Mrs Cowdray of Rose Hill Road, Wandsworth, in south London. At this point she wrote to her father seeking to patch up their quarrel. Her father wrote back in friendly terms but did not receive a reply.

The reason was that Nichols had returned to drinking. In late July Nichols stole three pounds and ten shillings from her employers and then absconded, taking with her a quantity of clothing, most of which she sold, but one dress she kept and was wearing when she was murdered. She went first to the reasonably respectable Wilmott's Lodging House in Thrawl Street, Spitalfields, but soon moved on to the cheaper and far less respectable White House at Flower and Dean Street. She was by this point working as a prostitute again and may have been attracted by the White House's policy of allowing men and women to share beds without requiring them to be married.

On the evening of 30 August she went out looking for clients, but when she returned to the White House just after midnight she had no money at all. The manager told her she could not stay without paying, so she went out again. Her final words were 'Never mind! I'll soon get my doss money. See what a jolly bonnet I've got now.' She was, indeed, wearing a new black bonnet that nobody had seen her with before. At 2.30 am another White House resident, Emily Holland, met Mary Ann on the corner of Whitechapel Road and Osborn Street. Holland noticed that Mary Ann was drunk and staggering. Holland asked if she was all right, to which Nichols replied that she had earned her bed money, but had spent it all on drink so she was penniless again. Holland pointed out the time, and Mary Ann told her to go home, adding: 'It won't be long before I'm back.' That was the last time that Mary Ann Nichols had been seen before her body was discovered an hour and 15 minutes later.

A MASS KILLER IS SUSPECTED

The police questioned everyone who had known Nichols or who had had contact with her in the last days of her life. They found nobody who could even remotely be thought to have a reason to kill her. As with Martha Tabram they were left with the conclusion that she had been killed by a male client that she had picked up just minutes before she was murdered. There were other similarities between the two deaths. Both bodies had been left arranged as if they were having sex, both had their skirts lifted up to reveal the groin and abdomen and both had suffered multiple knife wounds to the lower abdomen and groin area.

Osborn Street, formerly called Dirty Lane, and, where it joins Brick Lane, the scene of the attack on Emma Smith: this was only a short walk away from where Nichols' body was found.

There was also the matter of where the murders had taken place. Both women had been killed in places where passers-by could be expected to appear at any moment. Indeed, PC Neil came across Nichols' body within a few minutes of her death. And both murder scenes were located just feet from where people were sleeping, and the killing was committed without enough noise to wake them up. Moreover both killings had been committed in side streets just north of the Whitechapel Road, less than half a mile apart. And both murders had been committed at the weekend within four weeks of each other.

For the police investigating the two murders, the conclusion was inescapable. The two women had been murdered by the same man. This was a disturbing thought. The vast majority of killings in 19th-century Britain fell into one of two categories. Either a person was murdered in cold and deliberate fashion by somebody who knew them and had a reason for wanting them out of the way, or they were killed in the heat of the moment during a fight or a robbery. In either case, the murders were one-off events. The killer had not killed before and, assuming he or she was not caught and hanged, did not appear to kill again. Of course there had been a few rare instances of a person murdering more than once. But apart from their multiple killings they more or less fitted the usual pattern for British murderers.

PREVIOUS 19TH-CENTURY MASS KILLERS

In 1888 the most recent example of a mass killer was Mary Ann Cotton, who had been hanged in 1873. Cotton had been born into a working class family in the coalfields of County Durham. At the age of 20 she married William Mowbray and had five children, four of whom died in infancy. Mowbray died after 13 years of marriage, his widow collecting the equivalent of six months' wages in life insurance. Within weeks the widow had married again, to another man who fell ill and died leaving his wife to collect a hefty life insurance. She then moved to Sunderland and married a third husband whose children then died, along with Mary Ann's mother who had moved in with them. When this third husband, James Robinson, discovered that his wife had amassed huge debts in his name without telling him he threw her out. Mary Ann then moved to Northumberland where she 'married' a fourth time, to Frederick Cotton, though this new husband, his sister and three of his children all died fairly quickly with their lives well insured. Mary Ann did not bother marrying her next lover, but simply moved in with him. A few weeks later he too had died along with his son by Mary Ann.

At this point Frederick Cotton's fourth son who had somehow survived died suddenly. The parish clerk, Thomas Riley, knew the boy well and was convinced that he had been in the peak of health. Riley went to the doctor who had attended the boy, and both then went to the police. The police exhumed the body and tests found it contained a lethal amount of arsenic. Mary Ann Cotton was arrested and in March 1873 went for trial. She was found guilty of the murder of young Cotton and hanged. Reasoning that there was no point spending the money, the police did not investigate the other deaths that had followed Mary Ann Cotton. However, they estimated that she had murdered between 15 and 21 people.

Horrific as this body count is, the motives for the deaths were quite simple. Cotton murdered them for their money and for the money she got in life insurance.

The other notorious mass killer of 19th-century Britain had been William Palmer, hanged in 1856. Palmer came from a wealthy Staffordshire family and trained as a doctor in London. He lost his first job when suspected of stealing, after which he returned to Staffordshire. He promptly began a relationship with an attractive young woman, whose husband died after eating a meal with Palmer. When that romance ended, Palmer married Ann Thornton who stood to inherit a fortune when her widowed mother died. Two years later Ann's mother died while visiting her daughter and son-in-law, leaving her money to the young couple. Over the next five years four of Palmer's five children died, followed by Ann, all of their lives having been well insured. The following year Palmer's brother died, also well insured, followed by Leonard Bladen to whom Palmer owed a large sum of money.

In November a local bookmaker friend of Palmer's, John Cook, died suddenly after having a meal with Palmer. The large sums of money he was known to have in his house vanished, along with betting slips that were known to exist showing that Palmer owed him money. Cook's father demanded an investigation, as a result of which Palmer was arrested for Cook's murder. Uncertain that they could secure a conviction on the evidence they found about Cook's death, the authorities exhumed the bodies of Palmer's wife and brother, both of which contained large amounts of poison. In the event, Palmer was found guilty of the murder of Cook and hanged. He was generally thought to have murdered eight people. Again his motive was greed, pure and simple.

PANIC IN WHITECHAPEL

The detectives investigating what were quickly being termed the Whitechapel murders were clearly grappling with a very different sort of a killer. Both Tabram and Nichols had been poor to the point of destitution. When Nichols had spoken to Emily Holland just an hour before her death she had said that she had spent all her money on drink. Clearly robbery was not the motive. As for personal motives, the only link between Tabram and Nichols that police could find was that they were street prostitutes. They had not known each other, nor did they have any acquaintances in common. There were simply no links between the two. Every link the police tried to follow led to a dead end. It looked as if the two women had been chosen at random by a man intent on murdering someone, anyone.

The fact that there was no obvious motive was not lost on the residents of Whitechapel. As early as 2 September a rumour was going round that a murderous lunatic was on the loose. People began to look for such a person. Mental illness was, at this date, poorly understood and the idea of insanity was restricted to those who were clearly mentally incapable. Others suffering mental health issues were deemed to be simple, slow or just odd. People believed that a man insane enough to commit brutal murders of unexampled savagery in public places would be obviously insane. It was also presumed that the killer would be drenched in blood from the wounds inflicted on the victims. No such person as a gibbering lunatic covered in blood could be found. Combined with the speed and silence with which the killer clearly operated, this made the murders all the more unnerving.

A BAD CASE OF NERVES?

The fact that people were jumpy is shown by two incidents on the evening of 1 September. A man named Henry Birch ran a milk stall at the entrance to Little Turner Yard. At about 11.15 pm a man wearing a blue serge suit and a low-crowned hat and carrying a large cloth bag came up and bought a glass of milk. While he was drinking the milk, the man kept glancing about as if looking for someone and acted in a very furtive manner. When he handed back his glass, the man asked Birch if he could step into the yard for a few minutes. Birch did not own the yard, so he nodded. After several minutes there was no sign of the man, so Birch himself went into the yard. He found the man now hatless and changed into a set of clean overalls. He jumped in alarm when he saw Birch and crammed something into his bag.

'That was a terrible murder last night, wasn't it?' the man said. Then he grabbed his bag, pushed past Birch and ran off along Commercial Road towards Whitechapel High Street.

Birch at once shut up shop and hailed a nearby policeman. He was convinced that he had seen the killer, reasoning that the man had changed into overalls to protect his clothes from the spurting blood of his next victim. Birch and the policeman set off towards Whitechapel High Street, gathering helpers as they went, all looking for a man in overalls carrying a bag. They never found him, but the search lasted some time and caused quite a disruption in the area.

That same night a man in a pub in Whitechapel began asking questions about the murders, wanting to know details of the cuts and injuries inflicted. Having pestered several people, he left. Once he was gone the barman thought he had behaved oddly, guessed he might be the killer and again began a fruitless search.

Meanwhile, the man seen by the railway signalman Ede had been identified. He turned out to be a local man named Henry James. He was generally reckoned to be 'a bit simple in the head' but to be utterly harmless. In any case the police quickly found where he had been on the night of the Tabram murder and so eliminated him from their inquiries.

On 2 September the coroner, Wynne Baxter, opened his inquest into the death of Mary Ann Nichols. After hearing enough evidence to conclude that the woman was dead, had been murdered and that there was no likely suspect, Baxter adjourned the hearing. Dr Llewellyn gave limited evidence in public, and rather more graphic details of the injuries inflicted on the woman in private.

SCOTLAND YARD TAKES OVER

The short hearing saw the arrival in Whitechapel of Inspector Frederick Abberline of Scotland Yard. He told Baxter that the case had been taken over by Scotland Yard and that he was leading the investigation. It was a clear sign that the police were taking the killings very seriously indeed. Abberline was born in 1843 in Dorset and apprenticed to a clockmaker. But at the age of 20 he went to London and joined the police. After two years on the beat he was promoted to sergeant, then was quickly transferred to the CID. There he was given the tricky task of investigating the Irish terrorists then carrying out murders and planting bombs as part of a campaign to achieve an independent Ireland. After success in this task he was in 1878 put in charge of the Whitechapel CID where he remained until 1887, when he was promoted to be Inspector First Class and transferred to Scotland Yard.

By August 1888, Abberline was reckoned to be one of the most tenacious and systematic of the detectives at Scotland Yard. If he did not go in for inspired guesswork or dashing about in fast cabs, he did excel at thorough study of the minutest clues. It was this, combined with his knowledge of Whitechapel, that caused him to be put in charge of the Tabram–Nichols investigation.

The next day Baxter's inquiry continued with evidence from the police, and from Charles Cross and Robert Paul who had first found the body and then gone in search of a policeman. Residents of the White House lodging house also appeared. The inquiry was then adjourned for a fortnight to allow the police to gather more evidence.

By 5 September, opinion on the streets was turning away from the idea that a lone lunatic was responsible. A rumour ran round Whitechapel that a respectable working class woman had been attacked in a side street off Brick Lane the night before. It was said that the woman had been engaged in conversation by a well dressed man, then suddenly grabbed from behind and dragged into an alley. There three other men held her firm while the first man began going through her pockets and pulling the rings off her fingers. When the woman struggled to break free, one man produced a knife and held it to her throat, hissing in malevolent tones: 'Keep still, or I'll serve you the way I did the others.' Robbed of all her valuables, the woman was pushed to the ground while the gang ran off.

The tale prompted a general belief that the killings were being carried out by a particularly ruthless gang of street thieves. Others did not believe the tale. They pointed out that the prospect of being hanged would mean it very unlikely that a gang would dare operate in such a way. It was confidently predicted that sooner or later one member of the gang would get frightened and go to the police to save his own neck. Indeed, some of the tougher men in Whitechapel who might be expected to know how

Chief Inspector Frederick Abberline as he appeared at the time of the murders. Abberline was sent to take charge of the investigation after the murders of Nichols and Tabram were linked.

groups of criminals behave were the most vociferous in denying that the killings had been done in this way.

When the police heard of the stories, they announced that no such attack on a woman had taken place, which stopped the rumours. The idea of a lone madman reasserted itself.

By this date it was also noticeable that the numbers of people on the streets of Whitechapel after dark had increased dramatically. The reason was that respectable women were refusing to go out alone after dark. Those that worked late shifts, or had to be at work early in the morning, were insisting that husbands, fathers, brothers or boyfriends walk them through the streets. There were, therefore, very few women walking alone as most of them were accompanied by a man. And those men then had to complete their journey alone, adding to the numbers of people walking about the streets. Some were of the opinion that with all these people walking about, it would prove impossible for the killer to strike again.

The *East London Advertiser* spoke for many when its editorial column on 8 September declared:

The cunning of the lunatic, especially of the criminal lunatic, is well-known; but a lunatic of this sort can scarcely remain at large for any length of time in the teeming neighbourhood of Whitechapel. The terror which, since Thursday last, has inspired every man and woman in the district, will keep every eye on the watch. A watch should be kept indeed behind the windows in every street in Whitechapel. The murderer must creep out from somewhere; he must patrol the streets in search of his victims. Doubtless he is out night by night. Three successful murders will have the effect of whetting his appetite still further, and unless a watch of the strictest be kept, the murder of Thursday will certainly be followed by a fourth. The whole of East London is directly interested in bringing the assassin to justice. Every woman in those parts goes in nightly danger of her life as long as he remains at large. In one respect, no doubt, the crowded character of that quarter of the metropolis provides a certain safety for criminals of all kinds; but in a case like this where every inhabitant is bound, from motives of mere personal safety, to become a sort of unauthorized detective, continuously on the alert, the chances of a murderer's escape are fewer than they would be in a more thinly populated region.

On 6 September Mary Ann Nichols was buried. The event was reported in the *Evening Standard* as follows:

The funeral of Mary Ann Nichols, who was murdered in Buck's row last Friday, took place yesterday at Ilford. The arrangements were of a very simple character. The time at which the cortege was to start was kept a secret, and a ruse was perpetrated in order to get the body out of the mortuary, where it had lain since the day of the murder. The mourners were Mr. Edward Walker, father of the deceased, and his grandson, together with two of the deceased's children. The procession proceeded along Baker's row and past the corner of Buck's row into the main road, where police were stationed every few yards. The houses in the neighbourhood had the blinds drawn, and much sympathy was expressed for the relatives.

If some hoped that the funeral marked an end to the horror, they were soon to be proven sadly mistaken.

CHAPTER 6:

VICTIMS AND INFORMERS

S uspicion is a terrible thing. As the body count in Whitechapel began to rise, the population of the East End started to believe that the killer could very well turn out to be a member of their community. Soon informers and passers-by were coming forward to tell police of men acting strangely, men with knives, men turning violent, and men behaving suspiciously. Arrests were frequent and grudges led to many innocent men being locked away. Yet still the killer walked free.

VICTIM NUMBER THREE IS DISCOVERED

The poor, mutilated body of Mary Ann Nichols had been buried less than 48 hours when the *London Evening News* hit the streets with a terrifying headline:

ANOTHER EAST END MURDER.
A WOMAN'S THROAT CUT AND HER BODY RIPPED OPEN.

Given that this was just hours after the body had been found the details available to the *Evening News* were sparse, but there was enough to cause alarm.

> *About a quarter to six this morning the body of a woman was found behind a door in a backyard in Hambro-street off Brick-lane, Spitalfields. Her throat, as in the Whitechapel murder, was cut,*

and her body ripped down the front. The similarity of this to the
preceding murders leads us to believe they are all the work of one
man. The affair has created immense excitement in the district.

The body had been found at 5.45 am on Saturday 8 September by
John Davis, a 56-year-old cart driver who lived on the third floor of 29
Hanbury (not Hambro) Street, Whitechapel, along with his wife and
three adult sons. At 5.45 am he got up to go to work, hearing the bells of
the local church chiming as he did so. He went downstairs to the passage
that not only gave access to the staircase, but also to the backyard. The
front door was wide open, the back door shut. Davis went to the back
door, apparently intending to go to the toilet at the end of the yard before
heading off to work. Lying prostrate on the ground close to the back step
was the body of a woman, blood and gore covering the ground nearby.

In no doubt that he had found another body, Davis bolted out of the
front door to find a policeman. He found instead two men standing
outside Bayley's Packing Case shop five doors down. Davis told the men
what he had found and persuaded them to follow him into the passage
and stand at the back door to guard the body until he fetched the police.
He then ran to Commercial Street Police Station to report the dead body.
Having led the police back to No. 29 he went to work.

Meanwhile the two passers-by Davis had dragged into the murder
scene – James Green and James Kent – had been joined by a third man,
Henry Holland, who had seen Davis running off at top speed and had
come in to see what was going on. The three men peered at the body, but
did not touch it or do anything else. After a few minutes a pair of police
constables turned up to take over, and the three men left. Kent, a youth
barely out of his teens, was badly shaken by the state of the body. He
went to the Black Swan pub further down Hanbury Street and bought
himself a stiff whisky before returning to work.

By the time Kent got back to work a small crowd had gathered outside No. 29, being held back by a pair of burly policemen. Although Kent did not know it, Inspector Joseph Chandler was inside and Inspector

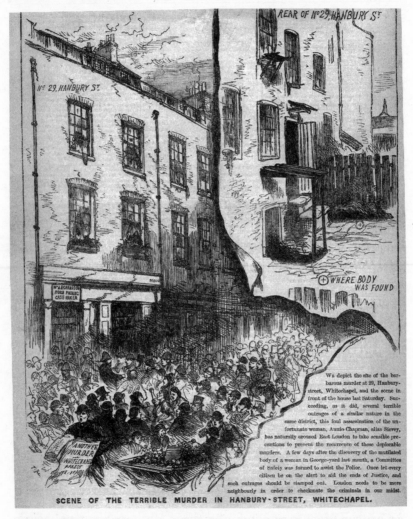

We depict the site of the barbarous murder at 29, Hanbury-street, Whitechapel, and the scene in front of the house last Saturday. Succeeding, as it did, several terrible outrages of a similar nature in the same district, this foul assassination of the unfortunate woman, Annie Chapman, alias Sievey, has naturally aroused East London to take sensible precautions to prevent the recurrence of these deplorable murders. A few days after the discovery of the mutilated body of a woman in George-yard last month, a Committee of Safety was formed to assist the Police. Once let every citizen be on the alert to aid the ends of Justice, and such outrages should be stamped out. London needs to be more neighbourly in order to checkmate the criminals in our midst.

SCENE OF THE TERRIBLE MURDER IN HANBURY-STREET, WHITECHAPEL.

Hanbury Street was packed with an immense crowd on the day after the killing, with residents charging a penny a time for people to enter and see the scene of the third murder.

Abberline had been sent for. Also present was Dr George Bagster Phillips, who lived locally and had been brought by the police. He later described what he found:

On Saturday last I was called by the police at 6.20 a.m. to 29, Hanbury-street, and arrived at half-past six. I found the body of the deceased lying in the yard on her back, on the left hand of the steps that lead from the passage. The head was about 6in in front of the level of the bottom step, and the feet were towards a shed at the end of the yard. The left arm was across the left breast, and the legs were drawn up, the feet resting on the ground, and the knees turned outwards. The face was swollen and turned on the right side, and the tongue protruded between the front teeth, but not beyond the lips; it was much swollen. The small intestines and other portions were lying on the right side of the body on the ground above the right shoulder, but attached. There was a large quantity of blood, with a part of the stomach above the left shoulder. I searched the yard and found a small piece of coarse muslin, a small-tooth comb, and a pocket-comb, in a paper case, near the railing. They had apparently been arranged there. I also discovered various other articles, which I handed to the police. The body was cold, except that there was a certain remaining heat, under the intestines, in the body. Stiffness of the limbs was not marked, but it was commencing. The throat was dissevered deeply. I noticed that the incision of the skin was jagged, and reached right round the neck. On the back wall of the house, between the steps and the palings, on the left side, about 18in from the ground, there were about six patches of blood, varying in size from a sixpenny piece to a small point, and on the wooden fence there were smears of blood, corresponding to where the head of the deceased laid, and immediately above the part where the blood had mainly flowed from the neck, which was well clotted.

A FAMILIAR PATTERN EMERGES

Even before an autopsy had been done, the similarities to the earlier killings were clear. The victim was a middle-aged woman, probably a prostitute, who had been killed with a knife and horribly mutilated. The body had been placed as if she were having sex, her skirts pulled up and her abdomen and groin horribly cut about. When the autopsy was carried out, by the same Dr Phillips, it revealed that this time the killer had gone much further in his mutilations and brutality.But in one key respect the murder was identical to that of Nichols, though not of Tabram. There were bruises to the jaw and upper throat that had been caused by great pressure from strong hands. The killer appeared to have grabbed the woman by the throat and half-strangled her into submission before killing her by cutting her throat. The bloodstains on the fence indicated that the killer had lowered the presumably unconscious woman to the floor before cutting her throat, and then mutilating the body.

As before, the basic tasks confronting the police were first to question everyone in the area to find out what they had seen or heard, and second to discover the identity of the dead woman.

First to be questioned were the residents of 29 Hanbury Street and neighbouring properties. They were rounded up by Inspector Chandler and taken to the Commercial Street Police Station for questioning, which went on for three hours.

Amelia Richardson, a widow, and her grandson Thomas lived on the first floor of the house, sleeping in the front room. The front of the ground floor was a workshop run by Mrs Richardson, assisted by her

37-year-old son John, who had his own rooms just around the corner, and a workman named Francis Tyler. Together they made packing cases that were then sold to various other shops in the area. On market days, John Richardson earned cash as a porter in Spitalfields Market just a few yards away at the west end of Hanbury Street. The cellar and backyard were also rented by Mrs Richardson, who used them for storage.

Saturday 8 September was a market day, so John was due to be up early to go to the market. However, there had been a break-in to the cellar storeroom a few weeks earlier and some tools were stolen. John was in the habit of checking the storeroom on market days. At about 4.45 am he had called at 29 Hanbury Street, walking through the passageway and out on to the back step. From there he had looked into the yard and had seen that the entrance to the cellar was firmly locked. He had then sat on the back step to cut from his boot a piece of leather that had come loose and was annoying him.

KILLER STRIKES AT DAWN

At this time the dawn had not yet broken, but the pale grey light of the pre-dawn was creeping up. John Richardson was absolutely clear that if there had been a body in the yard he would have seen it. That put the time of death at between 4.45 am and 5.45 am. Amelia Richardson said that she had been asleep all this time and had heard nothing. The other residents were no more helpful. The attic was occupied by the widowed Mrs Cox, who was asleep and heard nothing. The rear of the first floor was occupied by the Copsey sisters, who were also asleep. Potentially the most useful resident was Mr Waker who occupied the rear room on the ground floor with his mentally retarded teenage son. The Wakers habitually slept with their window slightly open. That window looked out on to the murder scene and was no more than 14 feet from where the woman had died. But Mr Waker had similarly heard nothing. Once again, it seemed, the killer had struck in total silence.

Or perhaps not. Living at No. 27 was a carpenter named Albert Cadosch – and he had heard something. Cadosch had got up to go to work and heard the church clock strike 5.15 am as he dressed. Once dressed he went out to the backyard to go to the toilet. As he left his back door he was aware that one or more persons were moving in the yard of No. 29. He heard a woman say 'No'. He thought nothing of it and went on to the toilet. When he had finished he walked back to his house, but then needed to suddenly go to the toilet again. As he returned to the back door a second time, he 'heard a sort of a fall against the fence', but again took little notice as the backyard of No. 29 not only contained their toilet but was also used by Mrs Richardson and her helpers in her packing case business. The fence was six feet tall and made of wooden palings, so he could not see through it and did not bother to look over it. Cadosch walked on through his house and out into the street to go to work.

The possessions on the body held no clue to the woman's identity. She had been wearing a long black coat, a black skirt, brown bodice, two petticoats, red and white striped woollen stockings, lace-up boots and a neckerchief tied three-cornered around her neck. Among her possessions were a scrap of muslin, two combs and a corner of an envelope containing two pills. The envelope was a potential clue, as it had on it the seal of the Sussex Regiment and a stamp postmarked 'London, 28, Aug., 1888', though the address was missing.

SWARMS OF SIGHTSEERS

Meanwhile, events on the streets were gathering pace. In Hanbury Street itself a sizeable crowd had gathered by around 8 am, growing and shrinking as people joined and left but never dispersing. By 11 am the police allowed the residents of No. 29 back, but they kept the backyard sealed off with a constable on duty at the back door to stop anyone gaining access. Mr Waker proved to be an enterprising man. By noon he was charging people a penny a time to come into his bedroom and look out of the window at the yard, complete with profuse bloodstains. Equally quick off the mark was a baker who by lunchtime was selling hot pies from a barrow to the crowd in Hanbury Street. He was soon joined by two costermongers selling fruit.

At 11.45 a great cry went up from the people at the western end of Hanbury Street. 'The murderer is caught,' the people shouted. The crowd at once surged along the street, pouring out into Commercial Street and congregating around the police station there. The crowd jostled around, shouting out to know what was going on and demanding entry to the station. After a while a police sergeant came out and shouted for silence. He then announced that a man had been arrested for picking pockets and that he had nothing to do with the killings. The crowd then gradually dispersed, with many people going back to Hanbury Street while others remained at the police station waiting for more news.

Then came news that a woman had been found with her throat cut in the churchyard of St Philip's Church in Stepney Way off the south side of Whitechapel Road. The crowd streamed east to reach St Philip's. The vicar there had to climb on to the wall to be heard as he shouted out that no dead body had been found on the premises. The first arrivals departed, but as the rumour spread more and more people came to St Philip's demanding to be shown where the body had been found. By 1 pm the vicar had given up and summoned the police. A constable was put on the gates to turn people away and assure them that no new murder had been committed.

Most workers had Saturday afternoon off, so by 2 pm the crowds surging around Hanbury Street, Commercial Street Police Station and the mortuary were immense. So densely were the crowds packed that policemen had trouble pushing their way through as they went on and off duty.

THE KILLER'S DESCRIPTION IS CIRCULATED

That afternoon a prostitute named Emily Walton pushed her way to the front of the crowd and asked to speak to a detective. She had, she said, information. She was taken to see Inspector Helson. She told him that at 2.30 am on the night of the murder she had been looking for a client in Hanbury Street when she was approached by a man. There was something about the man she did not quite like. He offered her two half sovereigns (gold coins worth ten shillings each) to go with him into a side alley. Given that her usual price was only sixpence, this was a huge fee and again aroused her suspicions. When she looked at the coins she realized that instead of being gold coins they were highly polished brass medals. At that point she told the man to go away and he slunk off in a furtive fashion. She had got a very good look at the man, gave Helson a description and said she would recognize him again without doubt.

At 8.20 pm Abberline issued a handbill to be posted around London and given out by policemen. It was based on Emily Walton's statement and read:

Commercial Street Station, 8.20 p.m. – Description of a man wanted, who entered a passage of the house at which the murder was committed, with a prostitute, at 2.0 a.m., on the 8th. Age 37, height 5ft 7in, rather dark beard and moustache. Dress – Short, dark jacket, dark vest and trousers, black scarf, and black felt hat. Spoke with a foreign accent.

ANNIE CHAPMAN IDENTIFIED WITH A PHOTO

The police were, meanwhile, out and about with a photo of the victim taken in the mortuary. It did not take them long to find out who she was. She was Annie Chapman, a woman living at Crossingham's Lodging House at 35 Dorset Street. Like the others she was a street prostitute who had been short of money. Over the next few days the police questioned everyone who had known Chapman, or who lived at Crossingham's and were able to put together a picture of her life and habits.

Chapman had been born Anne Smith in 1841, the daughter of a retired soldier who was working as a servant. She was the oldest in a family that included four girls and a boy, all of whom got on well together. In 1869 she married a coachman named John Chapman and settled in Bayswater, later following John's work to Windsor. The couple had two daughters and a son. In 1882 one of the girls died aged 12, and Anne suffered some sort of a breakdown. She took to heavy drinking and several times over the next three years was arrested on the streets of Windsor for being drunk and disorderly. In 1886 Anne and John separated, the children remaining with the father while Anne moved to London and continued to drink heavily. John sent Anne a weekly ten shillings by postal order by way of maintenance.

In the autumn of 1886 Anne moved in with a man named John Sivvey and adopted the name of Anne Sivvey for a while, though the couple were never married. At this time Anne was earning a living by doing crochet work and selling flowers on the street. At Christmas 1886 John Chapman died and the weekly ten shillings stopped arriving. John Sivvey left Anne as soon as the flow of money ceased and moved to north London. It was some time in 1887 that Anne took to living in common lodging houses and to prostitution as a way of raising money to pay for her drinking.

In May 1888 Anne picked up with a retired soldier named Edward Stanley whom she had known in Windsor. Stanley worked as a bricklayer's

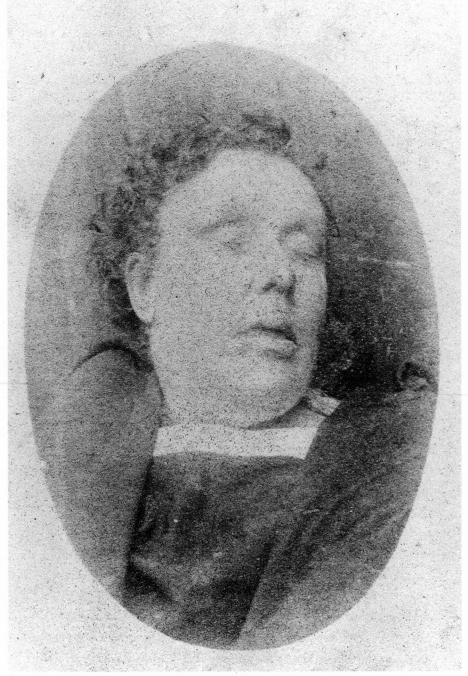

The mortuary photo of Annie Chapman that was taken the day after the murder and used by the police to identify the body.

mate and lived at 1 Osborn Place, Whitechapel. While Anne sometimes stayed with Stanley, she also frequented Crossingham's Lodging House. Stanley often paid for her bed at Crossingham's, and oddly also for that of another woman named Eliza Cooper.

Quite what the relationship was between Chapman, Cooper and Stanley is not entirely clear. What is known is that on 2 September the three of them, plus a street vendor named in newspaper reports only as 'Harry the Hawker', were drinking in the Britannia pub when an argument broke out between Chapman and Cooper. Stanley calmed the women down and took them back to Crossingham's. In the kitchen at the lodging house the argument broke out again, and this time the two woman began fighting with fists and kicks. John Evans, the night watchman, eventually managed to part the two, but not before Anne had got a black eye and some severe bruising.

The police spent some time questioning Cooper and Stanley over the argument and their relationships. Quite clearly Stanley and Cooper were reticent about discussing the argument – they gave quite different versions of what it had been about – and of how well they knew Chapman. The police were, however, satisfied that they had had nothing to do with the murder and let them go.

HAD JACK THE RIPPER BEEN SEEN?

From speaking to the other lodgers at Crossingham's the police were able to piece together Chapman's movements on the night she died. At 5 pm Amelia Palmer met Chapman in Dorset Street. Palmer lived at Crossingham's with her husband, who was unable to work properly after an accident at the docks and had a pension – she herself worked as a cleaner. She knew Chapman was a prostitute and asked her if she was going to Stratford to work that night. Chapman replied that she was not as she still felt ill, but then went on: 'It is of no use my going away. I shall have to go somewhere to get some money to pay my lodgings.'

She was next seen at 11.30 pm when she arrived at Crossingham's. She did not have any money to pay for a bed, but asked if she could sit in the kitchen for a while. The night watchman John Evans let her in. In the kitchen Anne persuaded another lodger, Frederick Stevens, to share a bottle of beer with her. He did not think she was drunk when he left her at about 12.15 am. A few minutes later William Stevens entered the kitchen and chatted to Chapman. He saw her take a box from her pocket, but it broke. She then took an envelope from the mantelpiece, tore it in half and put the pills from the box into one half, folded it and put that in her pocket – this was the envelope with the regimental crest found on her body. Chapman then left, presumably to get some money to pay for a bed for the night.

At 1.30 am she was back, but again was penniless. She was eating a baked potato that she had got from somewhere. This time she ignored Evans but went to see the manager Timothy Donovan, who was still awake. 'I haven't sufficient money for my bed,' she said, 'but don't let it. I shall not be long before I'm in.' Donovan then told her off about her drinking, saying she always seemed to have enough money for drink. Chapman did not respond to that but said, 'Never mind, Tim. I'll soon be back.' On her way out she told Evans, 'I won't be long. See that Tim keeps the bed for me.' She then went out, heading towards Spitalfields Market.

One final witness to Chapman's movements came forward later. This was Elizabeth Long who lived in Church Row, Whitechapel, with her husband James Long, a cart driver. She worked in Spitalfields Market and so her route to work took her down Hanbury Street. Although she did not know Chapman at all, she recognized the face in the mortuary photo as that of a woman she had passed on the morning of the murder. She had seen a man and a woman talking to each other close to 29 Hanbury Street. As she passed them the man said, 'Will you?' and the woman replied, 'Yes'. Long then passed on and arrived at work just after 5.30 am, putting her sighting of Chapman and a man at around 5.28 or so.

This created a slight time discrepancy with Cadosch who had heard what seems to have been Chapman and the killer in the backyard of No. 29 at about 5.22 am. However, neither Long nor Cadosch had a watch and were judging the time by the striking of church clocks, so one or other of them may have made a mistake of a few minutes in their guesswork.

Assuming Long was right, she had seen the killer, though only from behind. She said of him:

I noticed that he was dark. He was wearing a brown low-crowned felt hat. I think he had on a dark coat, though I am not certain. By the look of him he seemed to me a man over forty years of age. He appeared to me to be a little taller than the deceased. He looked like a foreigner. I should say he looked like what I should call shabby-genteel.

The description was not entirely different from that given by Emily Walton.

THE HUNT FOR 'LEATHER APRON'

The police, and the public, had meanwhile seized on the fact that a large leather apron had been found discarded in the yard of 29 Hanbury Street only feet from the dead body. It was found lying in a water trough, apparently having been scrubbed clean and then hastily abandoned. It was assumed that this explained how the killer managed to escape so easily after committing his crimes. While everyone had been looking for a lunatic drenched in blood, the killer had protected his clothes with this leather apron. The killer was at once dubbed 'Leather Apron', and as such was referred to by the press and the public alike.

The night of 9 September was a busy one for the police as they searched for Leather Apron. Before they had finished the police would have arrested no fewer than four men, one of whom turned out to be the man they sought.

The first arrest came at 6 pm in Deptford, when a woman approached a policeman and said that a man was acting suspiciously near the South Dock. The suspicious character turned out to be drunk and loudly looking for a prostitute. The policeman thought the man looked rather like the description of Leather Apron, so he arrested him and sent word to Inspector Abberline.

Just after 1 am a policeman patrolling down Buck's Row, where Nichols had been murdered, saw a man crouched in a badly lit corner. The policeman shone his lantern on the figure, revealing a man he later described as 'a villainous-looking fellow, with long hair and shaggy beard, dressed only in a pair of ragged blue serge trousers and an old dirty shirt'.

As soon as the lantern light struck him, the man fled. He ran to Brady Street, turning right into Whitechapel Road. The policeman gave chase shouting 'Leather Apron'. As the fugitive entered Whitechapel Road two passers-by leapt at him. The man fought back, kicking and trying to wriggle free, but was wrestled to the ground. He was hauled off to Bethnal Green Police Station with a small crowd following in his wake.

A little over an hour later, a policeman on patrol in Gloucester Street came across a man matching the description of Leather Apron. He asked the man to accompany him to Commercial Street Police Station. The man was then arrested and held for questioning.

None of these men turned out to be Leather Apron. The man in Deptford and the one from Gloucester Street were sailors who had only recently arrived in London. The man in Buck's Row also had a firm alibi, but he was wanted for questioning about a burglary in Kensington, so the police could claim some credit.

In any case, on the morning of 10 September Police Sergeant William Thick was a man on a mission. He not only knew who Leather Apron was, but he knew where Leather Apron was hiding. John Pizer, to give Leather Apron his real name, was a nuisance on Thick's patrol patch. A petty criminal prone to violence against women, he had gained his nickname from his habit of wearing a cobbler's leather apron, pretending to be an honest cobbler.

Sergeant Thick went to 22 Mulberry Street, Whitechapel, arriving at 8 am. He knocked and was unsurprised when Pizer's brother opened the door. Thick demanded to talk to John Pizer, but the brother denied that he was there. Thick pushed past the elder brother to find John Pizer cowering in a corner of the kitchen. Pizer begged Thick to go away, but Thick arrested him on suspicion of murder. As Thick started dragging Pizer towards the door, Pizer collapsed in tears saying that he would be torn apart by a mob if he set foot outside the door. Thick picked up a hat and gave it to Pizer, telling him to pull it down over his face.

Less than five minutes later Pizer was being hustled through the door of Leman Street Police Station. A woman who was in the reception room stared at Pizer, then ran out of the building. Within five minutes a small crowd had gathered. Twenty minutes later more than a hundred people were outside and the police had locked the doors. Ten minutes after that Leman Street was entirely blocked. The crowd was angry, with men shouting that Leather Apron should be brought out so he could be lynched. A few began to throw stones.

A little past 9 am the sergeant in charge stepped out of the front door.

The men based at Leman Street Police Station photographed in the station yard the year before the murders.

He waved his arms at the crowd to appeal for quiet. He then forcefully told the crowd that he was wearing the uniform of Her Majesty and challenged the crowd to lay hands on it. At this point reinforcements of policemen marched in from Commercial Street Police Station, shouldered their way through the crowd and formed up in front of the station. The crowd began to disperse, but there were still a hundred or so people hanging around at noon.

That evening a crowd gathered in Mulberry Street in the hope that Pizer would return there. The local policeman saw them and summoned reinforcements. After a while it became clear Pizer had gone elsewhere to lie low and the crowd dispersed.

That same day the police received a visit from Mrs Fiddymont, landlady of the Prince Albert pub in Brushfield Street, just 200 yards from the scene of the murder. She said that at 7 am on the morning of the murder a very peculiar customer had come in, whom she had never seen before.

The man had spots of dried blood on his hands and a smear of blood on his neck, below the right ear. He had, Mrs Fiddymont said, behaved in a nervous and furtive manner. He bought a drink, gulped it down in one and then left hurriedly, heading towards the City. Mrs Fiddymont described the man as having 'eyes as wild as a hawk' and wearing 'a brown stiff hat, a dark coat, and no waistcoat. His shirt was light blue check and torn badly. He had a light moustache and short sandy hair.'

THE WHITECHAPEL VIGILANCE COMMITTEE IS FORMED

Also on 10 September a group of Whitechapel businessmen and shop owners met in a local pub to discuss the situation. They were concerned that the murders and the furore surrounding them were giving Whitechapel a bad name. They had noticed that clients outside Whitechapel would look at them askance and orders were dropping off. After some discussion they decided on two courses of action. First they would lobby the government to post a large reward for the capture of the killer. The local MP had already offered £100, but nothing had come of it. The businessmen reasoned that the murderous maniac lived somewhere and that his fellow residents must know that he was a bit odd, but were perhaps reticent about reporting a friend to the police. A cash reward would help overcome such reticence. A letter was accordingly sent to the Home Secretary, Henry Matthews.

The businessmen also decided to establish the Whitechapel Vigilance Committee. In imitation of the vigilants hired in richer districts, the committee would hire a number of burly local men to patrol the streets armed with clubs. It was thought that with private patrols in addition to the police constables the killer would find it impossible to be alone with a victim long enough to carry out a murder. To organize the patrols and collect the money needed from local businesses, the men elected builder

George Lusk to be chairman and Joseph Aarons to be treasurer. Within two days the first patrols were out and about in Whitechapel at night.

The police were still hard at work and on 11 September made a discovery in the backyard of 25 Hanbury Street. On the fence were some smears of blood, while thrown into a corner was a piece of paper that was heavily bloodstained and screwed up. They concluded that the killer had wiped his hands on the paper to get rid of bloodstains, then thrown it into the yard.

That same day another man was arrested, not on suspicion of being the killer but for causing a public nuisance. John Brennan, a labourer aged 39, had gone into a pub in Camberwell, south London, and started talking about the murders in a macabre and obsessive fashion. He had shown some customers a knife, saying it was the murder weapon and proclaimed to anyone who would listen that 'Leather Apron' was a friend of his. This caused such a disturbance that the landlady locked herself in her private rooms. Two women in the pub ran out into the street, found PC Pillow on patrol and brought him to the pub. The constable instructed Brennan to leave, but he refused and was then arrested. When he appeared in court, Brennan said it had all been a joke that had gone too far and was bound over to keep the peace.

UNSPEAKABLE MUTILATIONS

On 12 September, the coroner's inquest into Chapman was opened by Wynne Baxter. The first day was taken up with evidence from inhabitants of 29 Hanbury Street and from the police. It was the next day that Dr Phillips gave a detailed account of how he believed Chapman had been killed. He added that the body had been subjected to 'further mutilations after death', then stopped reading from his report. The following exchange then took place:

The Coroner: *The object of the inquiry is not only to ascertain the cause of death, but the means by which it occurred. Any mutilation which took place afterwards may suggest the character of the man who did it. Possibly you can give us the conclusions to which you have come respecting the instrument used.*

The Witness: *You don't wish for details. I think if it is possible to escape the details it would be advisable. The cause of death is visible from injuries I have described.*

The Coroner: *You have kept a record of them?*

The Witness: *I have.*

The Coroner: *We will postpone that for the present.*

There were gasps from the public gallery, while reporters dashed out to push hurriedly scribbled notes into the hands of waiting telegram boys to be sent to their editors. Everyone knew from what had been said to reporters by Davis, Green, Kent and Holland that the body had been a mass of blood and that some internal organs had been lifted out and put beside the body. Quite clearly, however, the doctor had found something infinitely worse, something that was too horrible to mention in court. Word of the doctor's refusal to give details ran around London like wildfire. Whatever had been done to the body must have been terrible indeed.

Dr Phillips did, however, say that in his opinion the mutilations done to the body showed a fair degree of anatomical knowledge. He was also of the opinion that if he had attempted them himself it would have taken at least a quarter of an hour, possibly much longer. In fact Phillips and the police were reluctant to allow one particular piece of knowledge to be known to the public. The uterus, the upper portion of the vagina and most of the bladder had been cut out and taken away by the killer. No trace of them could be found.

ANOTHER FALSE ARREST

On 17 September a rumour ran around London that the police had caught the killer and that he was due to appear at Woolwich Magistrates' Court. Journalists poured into Woolwich to fill the press gallery, while the mass of people trying to get into the public gallery was immense. Sure enough at mid morning a man was brought before Mr Fenwick. He gave his name as Edward Quinn, labourer. His face was bruised and cut in a few places, while his clothes were bloodstained. He was charged with having been drunk the night before and with having committed the Whitechapel murders.

As the evidence unfolded the excitement in the courtroom gradually dispelled as it became obvious that the man was innocent. According to Quinn he had been walking from his home to a pub in Woolwich the previous night when he tripped over something in the pavement and banged his head heavily on a wall as he fell down. Although he had not realized it at the time, he had bled badly from the cut on his head and his clothes had got stained. After brushing himself down he went into the pub for a drink. Alarmed by his bloody appearance, the landlord had sent for a policeman who came and arrested Quinn.

According to the records the hearing ended with the following exchange.

Mr. Fenwick: *Were you not drunk?*
Quinn: *Certainly not, sir.*

Mr. Fenwick: *You will be remanded until tomorrow.*

Quinn: *This is rather rough. I am dragged a mile to the station, and locked up, and now I am to wait another day with all this suspicion of murder hanging over my head.*

Mr. Fenwick: *I will take your own bail in £5 for your reappearance.*

Quinn: *I object to the whole thing. Me murder a woman! I could not murder a cat (laughter).*

The police did not push the matter and Quinn walked free.

On the same day Coroner Baxter reopened his inquiry into the death of Mary Ann Nichols. Inspector Helson appeared to give a summary of the police actions to date, but had to admit that nothing had been found and no progress made. The foreman of the jury then asked if he could say a few words. Baxter agreed. The following exchange showed clearly how the murders and the lack of progress were being viewed on the streets of Whitechapel. According to the *Evening Standard*:

> The Foreman of the Jury said that if a substantial reward had been offered in the first case he believed that the last two murders would never have been perpetrated. If the matter was put before the Home Secretary, and a large reward was promised, he (the Foreman) would willingly give £25. Had the murdered persons belonged to the rich and aristocratic class, a reward would immediately have been offered.

Coroner Baxter at once told the foreman to sit down and declared that 'the Government cared just as much for the lives of the poor as for the lives of the rich'.

Baxter then summed up the evidence presented in the inquiry. He added that in his opinion a properly equipped public mortuary should be opened in Whitechapel as soon as possible, then asked the jury for their finding. The foreman replied:

Yes, sir. We are unanimously of the opinion that we should give an open verdict of Murder against some person or persons unknown, and we wish to thank you for your remarks with reference to the necessity for a mortuary, and for the very able way in which you have conducted the inquiry.

WHITECHAPEL ALMOST BACK TO NORMAL

By this time the police had increased the number of their patrols, while the Whitechapel Vigilance Committee patrols were similarly increasing in number. A reporter from the *Evening Standard* spent a night wandering the streets of Whitechapel, and found the area almost back to its old self. Next day he filed the following report:

The scare, which the disclosure of the fourth and most horrible of the murders occasioned in the district, has considerably subsided. People having become familiar with the details of the tragedy, and being calmed by the knowledge of the active measures adopted for their protection by the police, are returning to their normal condition of mind. This is plainly evidenced by the aspect which Whitechapel road presented on Monday night, and up to an early hour of the morning – a very different one from that of the corresponding period of the previous day. On Sunday night the pavements were almost deserted, but 24 hours later groups of men and women chatted, joked, and boisterously laughed upon the flagstones until long after St. Mary's clock struck one. In passing through the groups of people, the words most frequently heard in their conversation were 'Leather Apron.' The term has become a byword of the pavement and gutter, and one oftener hears it accompanied by a laugh than whispered in a tone which would indicate any fear of the mysterious individual who is supposed to live under that nickname. Whilst a large number of persons, including many members of the police force, believe in the guilt of 'Leather Apron,' the talk of the footways convinces the passer-by that a large number of other inhabitants of the East end are sceptical as to his personality. So it may be said with truth that the thoroughfares on Monday night presented their customary appearance. There was the usual percentage of gaudily dressed, loud, and vulgar women at the brightly lighted cross ways; and the still larger proportion of miserable, half fed, dejected creatures of the same sex upon whom hard life, unhealthy habits, and bad spirits have too plainly set their stamp. Soon after one o'clock the better dressed members of the motley company disappeared; but the poor wretches crawled about from lamp to lamp, or from one dark alley's mouth to another, until faint signs of dawn appeared. Off the main road – in such thoroughfares as Commercial street and Brick lane – there was little to attract attention. Constables passed silently by the knots of homeless vagabonds huddled in the recess of some big door way; other constables, whose plain clothes could not prevent their stalwart, well drilled figures from betraying their calling, paraded in couples, now and again emerging from some dimly lighted lane and passing their uniformed comrades with an air of profound ignorance.

But if things seemed back to normal, they weren't. As events would soon show.

CHAPTER 7:

JACK THE RIPPER

With three women murdered in almost identical fashion in less than five weeks, it was clear that a dangerous killer was on the loose and that, though there were thousands of rumours, no one had a clue who he was. Thus far the murderer had lacked a name, but all that suddenly changed when the police were sent a letter out of the blue that claimed to come from the killer. It was signed with an ominous, terrifying name that has gripped the popular imagination ever since: Jack the Ripper.

MORE SCARES, MORE ARRESTS

On 14 September 1888 the remains of Annie Chapman were laid to rest in conditions of secrecy as the police wanted to avoid disorder on the streets. The *London Evening News* carried the story:

The funeral of Annie Chapman, the last victim of the Whitechapel murderer, took place yesterday morning. The utmost secrecy was observed in the arrangements, and none but the undertaker, police, and relatives of the deceased knew anything about it. Shortly after seven o'clock a hearse drew up outside the mortuary in Montagu-street and the body was quickly removed. At nine o'clock, a start was made for Manor Park Cemetery; the place selected by the friends of the deceased for the interment but no coaches followed as it was desired that public attention should not be attracted. Mr. Smith and other relatives met the body at the cemetery, and the service was duly performed in the ordinary manner. The remains of the deceased were enclosed in a black-covered elm coffin, which bore the words, 'Annie Chapman, died September 8, 1888. Aged 48 years'.

The police had good reason to be concerned about the public reaction to the funeral. The series of murders still dominated life in Whitechapel and across the East End of London, and scares were frequent. On the evening of 12 September, a vigilant on duty near the Tower of London had been approached by a man who asked: 'Have you caught any of the Whitechapel murderers yet?' On being told that nobody had yet been caught, the man whipped out a knife with a blade about a foot long that he then waved about while shouting, 'This will do for them!' He then ran off. The startled guard gallantly gave chase, but could not keep up and lost the man near Dock Street. Ominously the man was heading towards Whitechapel.

Later that same evening a couple of men got involved in an argument outside a pub in Whitechapel. A passing policeman broke up the dispute, but one of the men remained aggressive and threatened to stab his opponent. The policeman arrested him and took him to the police station where he was searched and a large knife found on him. The man was short, fat and dark-haired, which did not match the description the police were working on. Nevertheless he had to prove his whereabouts on the nights of the murders before he was eliminated from inquiries.

On the day of the funeral there were other developments. The paper found in the backyard of No. 25 had been analysed and the blood was confirmed as being human. Meanwhile, Edward Stanley, 'the Pensioner', who had paid some of Annie Chapman's bills, vanished from his home without telling any of his acquaintances where he was going. A flurry of excitement that he might be on the run due to a guilty conscience was dispelled when he contacted the police to say he was moving about looking for work. Another person to turn up was Emma Potter, a teenage girl who had vanished from her family home a few days earlier and who was feared to have fallen victim to the killer. She had simply wandered off. Her mother was reported to be relieved to see her daughter, but unimpressed by her behaviour.

The police had also found a link between two of the murder victims. While tracing the large number of people who had stayed at Crossingham's Lodging House at the same time as Chapman they came across a name that they already knew: Mary Ann Connelly. Another prostitute, Connelly had not only shared a room with Chapman but had been the prostitute who was with Martha Tabram when they picked up two soldiers the night Tabram was murdered. This was considered important since it was still considered a possibility that the killer had a grudge against the women he had murdered, rather than having picked them at random. Where there was one link there might be more. Connelly was pulled in for questioning again.

Connelly gave Inspector Reid the name and address of a man who had known both Tabram and Chapman. Not only that but, as Reid spotted at once, the address was only two minutes' walk from Buck's Row where Mary Ann Nichols had been murdered. A man with a link to all three victims was clearly a prime suspect. Together with Detective Sergeant Enright and Sergeant Godley, Reid went round to question the man. However, he was quickly able to provide an alibi and witnesses to prove where he had been at the time of the murders. The new prime suspect had to be discounted almost as soon as he had been found.

EAST ENDERS BLAME THE AUTHORITIES

On 15 September the editor of the *Evening News* felt moved to write a strongly worded editorial in defence of the police. The people of the East End were worried, frightened and panic-stricken and many had written letters and signed petitions blaming the police or the Home Secretary for failures in hunting the madman who prowled their streets. The editor wrote:

> *The outcry, however, that is raised against the police because they have not arrested the actual murderer is unjust. No one can expect a police constable to be omnipresent; and it is no discredit to the force that one of its members did not happen to be on the spot at the precise moment when Annie Chapman was done to death in a back-yard in Hanbury-street. After the crime, the murderer vanished as completely as though he had never been, and left absolutely no trace of his existence, except the foul deed he had committed. There was not only no clue, there was no trace of a clue, no hint in what direction a clue was to be found, to guide the police. It was not so much that things were left vague and doubtful as that they were left absolutely blank. Under these circumstances it is inconsiderate folly to blame the police for not doing more than they have done. It is not too much to say that the highest intellects in the country would fail, just as does an ordinary constable or detective, to detect a criminal who leaves no tracks, unless the detection were more or less of an accident.*

The fact remained, however, that the police had not caught the man able to murder and mutilate in silence and apparently at will. The public remained alert and jumpy.

On 18 September Adelaide Rogers was standing alone in Down Street, Piccadilly, when she was approached by a man. The man suddenly attacked her, hitting her over the head before running off. The *Evening News* led the story with the words 'Another Terrible Outrage' and declared that the man had tried to cut her throat but that she had fought him off. But in later editions the newspaper had to retract after it became clear that no knife had been involved and that it was a simple robbery.

A REWARD IS OFFERED

The Whitechapel Vigilance Committee was still doing its work of collecting money from local businesses and hiring men to patrol the streets. On 19 September the secretary, Joseph Aarons, received a reply from the Home Office regarding their request for a large cash reward to be offered for information leading to the capture of the murderer. It read:

Sir – I am directed by the Secretary of State to acknowledge the receipt of your letter of the 16th inst. with reference to the question of the offer of a reward for the discovery of the perpetrators of the recent murders in Whitechapel, and I am to inform you that had the Secretary of State considered the case a proper one for the offer of a reward he would at once have offered one on behalf of the Government, but that the practice of offering rewards for the discovery of criminals was discontinued some years ago, because experience showed that such offers of rewards tend to produce more harm than good, and the Secretary of State is satisfied that there is nothing in the circumstances of the present case to justify a departure from this rule.

I am, Sir, your obedient servant,

G. Leigh Pemberton.

The Vigilance Committee was duly unimpressed and concluded that it was up to the people of Whitechapel to deal with the matter themselves. The following evening they held a large public meeting in a hall in Mile End Road with the sole purpose of publicizing and condemning the letter. There were several speakers, all agreeing that someone, somewhere must know the killer and have suspicions about his odd behaviour. The packed meeting ended with loud denunciations of the authorities and – to loud cheers – the announcement from Aarons that the Vigilance Committee was itself putting up £50 to add to the £100 already offered by the local MP.

The vicar of St Jude's, Whitechapel, wrote a long and thoughtful letter to *The Times* newspaper. He declared that the slaughter of the unfortunate women would have served a purpose

> *if at last the public conscience awakes to consider the life which these horrors reveal. The murders were, it may almost be said, bound to come; generation could not follow generation in lawless intercourse, children could not be familiarised with scenes of degradation, community in crime could not be the bond of society, and the end of all be peace.*

He went on to call for a greater police presence, better street lighting, improved street cleaning, the removal of slaughterhouses and other noxious industries from residential streets, clearance of the worst slum buildings and a tighter control by the civic authorities over what went on in his parish.

EVERYONE IS A SUSPECT

That same day a new arrest caused excitement as it involved a knife of the sort that the killer was thought to use. Alexander Feinberg of 51

Leman Street stopped at a stall selling coffee in Whitechapel Road on his way to work. He was roughly pushed aside by another man who appeared to be drunk. The stallholder told the new arrival to go away, whereupon Feinberg grunted his approval. The man then whipped out a long-bladed knife and lunged at Feinberg, who leapt aside. Other men at the stall then pounced on the knifeman and wrestled him to the ground. The beat policeman then appeared, handcuffed the man and frogmarched him off to the police station. He turned out to be Charles Ludwig, an unpleasant individual already wanted for assault. He was, however, not the killer.

On 26 September a man burst into Wandsworth Police Station in a state of great excitement. He announced that he had just been drinking in a pub with a man he worked with, plasterer-bricklayer's labourer John Fitzgerald, when he had confessed to being the Whitechapel murderer. The man knew that Fitzgerald could be aggressive when drunk, so the confession was not impossible. He quickly made his excuses and ran to get the police. Hurrying to the pub, the police found Fitzgerald had gone but since it was known he was living in common lodging houses it did not take long to find him.

Arrested and taken to the police station, Fitzgerald again confessed to the murder of Chapman, though not to the others. It was very obvious to the police, however, that the man was so drunk as to be almost incapable of standing. He was put in the cells until morning. Having sobered up, Fitzgerald withdrew the confession and hurriedly told police where he had been and who would back up his story. The police checked the alibi and got statements from the witnesses. Having established that Fitzgerald had been nowhere near Whitechapel when the murders took place they let him go again on 29 September 1888.

Meanwhile a lively correspondence was being conducted in *The Lancet*, the trade paper of the medical profession, on the subject of homicidal mania. The view of the medical establishment tended to be that a lunatic was not to blame. *The Lancet* summed this view up by stating: 'The theory that the succession of murders which have lately been committed in Whitechapel are the work of a lunatic appears to be by no means at present well established.'

Individual doctors working with the mentally ill were not so sure. Dr Forbes Winslow of Wimpole Street, who had the previous year interviewed at length one murderer subsequently declared insane, wrote: 'Homicidal lunatics are cunning, deceptive, plausible, and on the surface, to all outward appearance, sane; but there is contained within their innermost nature a dangerous lurking after blood which, though at times latent, will develop when the opportunity arises.'

By the end of the month the *Lancet* was calling for the authorities to crack down on 'immoral images' of a 'depraved character' that were used on theatre billboards or in shop windows to publicize shows and products. They reasoned that the bold display of pictures of women's ankles, low-cut tops and other provocative images might inflame the passions of passers-by and so play a role in precipitating the killings.

PANIC AT HOME AND ABROAD

The London newspapers continued to print anecdotes and incidents related to the murders. On 28 September the *Evening News* carried the following story from Ireland.

On Wednesday night a young girl named Duffy, residing with her parents in Chapel-street, Newry, ran home from a field in the suburbs of the town, where she had gone to fetch cows home for the night, and stated that she had been accosted by a strange man only partially dressed, who leaped out of a hedge and chased her through the field, saying he was 'Leather Apron,' and the murderer of the Whitechapel victims. When the girl reached home without waiting to bring the cows she was almost breathless and in a very excited state. Her father informed the constabulary of the affair, and they went to the field, but failed to find the mysterious stranger. An alarm of a similar kind has been exciting the minds of the people of Warrenpoint and the district for the past three or four days. So great is the panic amongst the female portion of the community that not one of them can be induced to go out on the Newry road after dark. The police believe the mysterious man is some half-crazy individual.

On 28 September a woman in Whitechapel was knocked to the ground after dark by a man who had first engaged her in conversation. She screamed and the man ran off. She gave a description of the man to the police, who failed to find him.

The following day a constable on his beat in Wandsworth found a disturbing chalk drawing on the pavement on St John's Hill. The first thing he saw was a very long chalk arrow on the pavement in Kingsland Road, pointing to the word 'Look!' Another arrow then led to the words 'I am Leather Apron. Five more, and I will give myself up'. Beneath this was a crude drawing of a man with a knife uplifted towards a woman. Having called his sergeant, the constable made a note of the markings, then rubbed them out so as to avoid causing worry among local residents.

A FOURTH SILENT KILLING

At 1 am on the morning of Sunday 30 September Louis Diemschutz was driving his pony and light cart up Berner Street. He turned into Dutfield's Yard intending to stable the pony and put the cart away, but the pony suddenly shied at something. There was no lighting in the yard and all Diemschutz could see was an object on the ground. He prodded it with his whip, then lit a match and saw it was a woman. Thinking she might be drunk or sick, Diemschutz went into the adjacent International Working Men's Educational Club to get help.

Diemschutz came back with Isaac Kozebrodsky, Morris Eagle and a candle. By the light of the candle they saw that the woman's throat was cut and a large pool of blood was covering the ground. The men at once ran out into the street shouting for the police. They ran off in different directions, and Eagle soon came back with constables Henry Lamb and Edward Collins. One look at the body was enough for Lamb. He sent Eagle running to Leman Street Police Station to fetch Inspector Reid, while Collins was sent to shut the club and keep everyone inside. Lamb then knelt down by the body. He found that it was still warm, that the blood had not completely congealed but that there was no sign of a pulse. He noticed that the body was arranged as the others had been, with the legs drawn up and apart as if for sex, but that the skirts had not been lifted and there were no obvious injuries to the abdomen or groin.

Lamb closed the gates to the yard to stop anyone coming in and searched every nook and cranny by the light of his lamp. Dr Frederick Blackwell then arrived and confirmed the woman was dead. Lamb had moved into the club and was methodically studying everyone's hands and clothes for spots of blood when Reid arrived.

Reid began by taking the names and addresses of everyone in the club, then questioned each briefly. As more and more policemen arrived, Reid sent them out to knock on all local doors to question the residents. It was very quickly obvious that the murder had only just taken place when Diemschutz had arrived. A meeting in the club had ended at 12.30 am and members had exited through the yard, none of them seeing anything. A Mrs Fanny Mortimer was standing on the front step of her house at

A contemporary view of the murder of Catherine Eddowes.

36 Berner Street that night. She watched the men leaving the meeting, heard the clock strike a quarter to one and then went inside to go to bed. The murder must therefore have happened between 12.45 am and 1 am. Diemschutz later said that he had got the impression that somebody else was in the dark yard along with the body, but since he had thought the woman was drunk he had taken no notice. The killing had also been done silently. A woman in the club had been sitting by a window overlooking the yard all this time and had heard nothing.

As usual the body gave no clues as to the woman's identity. There was a large pocket on the underskirt, which contained: a padlock key, a small pencil, six large buttons and one small, a comb, a broken comb, a spoon, a dress hook, a piece of muslin and two small pieces of paper. Reid sent the body off to the mortuary in the expectation that a photo of the woman's face would be taken in the morning, which would be used to identify the victim. Dr George Bagster Phillips, who had dealt with the Chapman autopsy, had arrived on the scene before the body was removed and would conduct the autopsy.

AND A FIFTH – TWO BODIES IN THE SAME NIGHT

While Inspector Reid was organizing the early stages of the investigation into the murder of the unknown woman in Berner Street, PC Edward Watkins was plodding his beat some 700 yards to the west, just over the border between Whitechapel and the City of London. The number of police on the streets had been so massively increased at night that beats were now taking only 15 to 20 minutes to complete. As Watkins turned into Mitre Square at 1.44 am, therefore, he was retracing the steps he had last taken at 1.28 am. At that point he had called in on George Morris, the night watchman on duty at the Kearley & Tonge Warehouse in the square. The two men had chatted briefly, and Morris had promised to make a brew of fresh tea for the next time Watkins came round in 15 minutes or so.

The square was small, barely 50 yards across. Before heading for his welcome cup of tea, Watkins shone his lamp to the left, then walked right and shone his lamp into the far corner beside an empty house. What he saw brought him rapidly to a halt. Lying on her back in the all too familiar position was a woman. Her skirts had been lifted up and her abdomen ripped open – blood and entrails were everywhere.

Watkins ran to the Kearley & Tonge Warehouse and pushed the door open, shouting: 'For God's sake, mate, come to my assistance!'

Morris was at his desk. He paused to get his own lamp asking, 'What's the matter?'

A sketch of the body of Catherine Eddowes showing the position of the body and organs – two pawn tickets found in a mustard tin were used to identify her.

'Oh dear,' Watkins said, 'there's another woman cut to pieces!'

The two men went back to the body. Watkins sent Morris off to fetch help while he stood back and used his lamp to study the body and its surroundings. It was a grisly task, but a necessary one. He could see nothing lying about that might be a clue. Morris was back inside five minutes with two more policemen, PC James Harvey and PC Holland, who had come running to his shouts for help. Holland was sent to fetch Dr George Sequeira and Inspector Edward Collard, who were on the scene by 2 am. Sequeira carried out a brief inspection of the body on the spot, estimating that she had been dead no more than 20 minutes and that death had been caused by the cutting of her throat. Dr Frederick Brown, the official police surgeon who arrived a couple of minutes later agreed.

As with the body found in Berner Street, the woman in Mitre Square had nothing on her to indicate who she was. Her clothes were dirty and poorly kept, which indicated that she was very poor, but beyond that not much could be deduced. Mitre Square was in the City of London, which meant it fell under the jurisdiction of the City Police, not the Metropolitan Police. It was to be a couple of hours before it was realized that two bodies had been found. Very quickly it was assumed that the killer had murdered in Berner Street, but had been disturbed by the arrival of Diemschutz before he could carry out the mutilations, and so had moved west to murder again.

THE KILLER LEAVES A TRAIL

But the night's horrors for the police were not over yet. PC Alfred Long was patrolling his beat and at 2.55 am was progressing down Goulston Street. As usual he glanced down the side alleys and into the various open doorways. At the entrance to the staircase that led to Nos 108 to 119 Model Dwellings (a block of tenements) his eye was caught by something that had not been there when he had last passed that way at about 2.25 am. He stepped into the entrance way and peered down at the object. It turned out to be a piece of cotton fabric, heavily drenched in blood and in places smeared with what seemed to be excrement. Having been on patrol since well before midnight, Long did not know that any new murders had taken place that night. Nevertheless the cloth was unusual enough for him to decide to go back to his police station to report it.

As Long turned to leave the stairwell he saw some chalk writing scrawled on the wall by the doorway. He got out his notebook and copied down what it said: 'The Juwes are the men that will not be blamed for nothing'. Long summoned Detective Constable Daniel Halse of the City of London Police to take over the strange finds. Halse did know about the murder in Mitre Square and was therefore interested in news of a bloodstained cloth. The killer had apparently wiped his hands clean on a piece of spare paper he had found after the murder in Hanbury Street, and this might be a repeat performance. Halse also made notes in his notebook, but he wrote down a slightly different version of the chalk writing: 'The Juwes are not the men who will be blamed for nothing'.

Halse also knew something else. The body from Mitre Square had been taken to Golden Lane Mortuary. Before Dr Frederick Brown could begin work on the body, it had first to be undressed. As this process went ahead it was found that the dead woman had been wearing a large white apron, but that it had been cut in half by a sharp knife and one half was missing. Halse carried the bloodstained cloth back to the mortuary and found it was the missing half. He at once sent Detective Hunt back to Goulston Street to begin the usual door knocking to question everyone in the area to find out if they had seen or heard anything unusual between 2.20 am and 2.55 am, the time period when the bloody apron had apparently been dropped. The rooms off the staircase where the apron was found were searched thoroughly, but nothing was found.

Attention then turned to the chalk writing. Whatever the precise wording of the writing, its meaning was clear. The person who wrote it thought that the Jews were guilty of something, but would escape the blame. Halse and Long were of the opinion that the writing was new. It was close enough to the doorway that it would have been rubbed and scuffed by people passing in and out. But it was not scuffed at all and so must have been written after the inhabitants had gone to bed in the hours leading up to midnight. They concluded that it had been written by the killer when he dropped the apron.

THE JEWS COME UNDER SUSPICION

The police already had two witnesses who thought they had seen the killer, and both said he had been 'foreign' in appearance. The suspect John Pizer, who had been released after his alibi proved firm, had been a Jew. The talk on the streets was of the opinion that no native Londoner would perpetrate such terrible crimes, and suspicion was falling heavily on the large number of new Jewish arrivals from eastern Europe. They had unfamiliar customs, spoke to each other in an incomprehensible language and did not integrate into the local community as earlier waves of immigrants had done. Moreover, Goulston Street had a population that was more than 50 per cent Jewish.

When Police Superintendent Thomas Arnold was told of the apron and writing he was at once alarmed. He was concerned that if word got out about the writing there might be an anti-Jewish riot. He sent a man to guard the doorway and refused to allow anyone to enter, then he sent a message to Sir Charles Warren, the Commissioner of the City Police.

Warren was just as worried as Arnold. He ordered that the writing should be washed off at once.

The misspelling of the word Jews as 'Juwes' would exercise the police greatly. At first it was thought that the spelling might be Russian or Polish, then that it might be Yiddish. After diligent enquiries among the immigrant Jewish community it was established that the spelling did not originate in any of these languages. French was suggested next, before being dismissed after checking with Frenchmen living in London. It was finally agreed that the writer was not fully literate and had simply spelled the word incorrectly.

THE LAST HOURS OF ELIZABETH STRIDE

It was the Metropolitan Police who identified their body first. A photo was taken of the dead woman and copies taken around Whitechapel by policemen who showed it to anyone who might have known a poor prostitute. The move paid off when a constable called at the common lodging house at No. 32 Flower and Dean Street – one of the roughest streets in Whitechapel. The deputy manager, Elizabeth Tanner, recognized the woman at once. She said she was a prostitute who had stayed, off and on, at the lodging house for the previous six years. The dead woman was a foreigner who went by the name of Long Liz, but Tanner did not know her real name. She was taken to the mortuary and positively identified the body.

Further questioning of residents at No. 32 produced several other people who recognized the body as that of 'Long Liz', but it was some hours before they discovered her real name: Elizabeth Stride. That information came from her regular lover, Michael Kidney of Devonshire Street. Kidney said that he shared his room with Stride, but that they had enjoyed an intermittent relationship due to her drinking. She

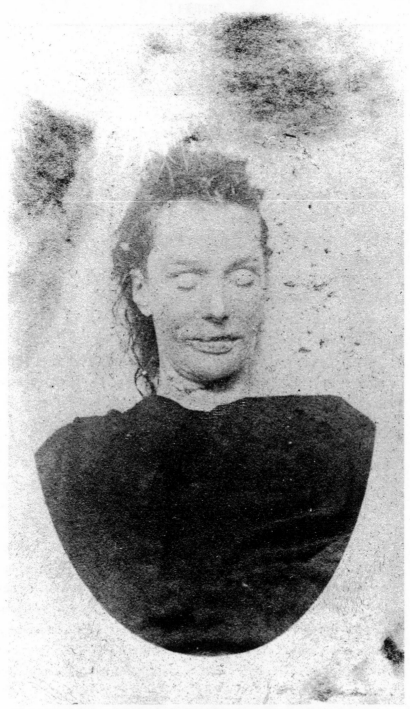

The mortuary photo of Lizzie Stride shows the body after the blood from the cut neck had been cleaned and her stained clothing replaced by a dark sheet.

would sometimes get drunk and then disappear for several days before returning again. He had last seen her on 25 September when he left for work in the docks. She had been sober and he expected her to be at home when he came back. The fact that she had gone did not surprise him, however, and he guessed she was off on a drinking spree. He gave the police some details of Stride's background, including the fact that she was Swedish and had come to London about 20 years earlier. That led police to the London Swedish community where they were able to learn about Stride's past.

Stride had been born near Gothenburg in Sweden in 1843, the daughter of a farmer named Gustaf Ericsson. By 1865 she was working as a prostitute in Gothenburg, but in 1866 made an effort to start afresh by taking a job as a housemaid with a Swedish family moving to London. In 1869 she left domestic service to marry John Stride, a carpenter from Sheerness. The couple separated in 1881, after which Stride told anyone who asked that she was a widow. She claimed that John had died in the sinking of the *Princess Alice*, a pleasure boat that went down in the Thames in 1878, and that she had been lucky to escape alive. Thereafter Stride had lived in lodging houses, settling in Flower and Dean Street by 1882, and working as a prostitute again. Her relationship with Kidney began in 1885.

By questioning her acquaintances, police discovered Stride's movements on the night she died. She had spent the afternoon cleaning the rooms at her lodging house to pay for her accommodation. She went out for a drink, returning at around 7 pm to give fellow resident Catherine Lane a large piece of new green velvet to look after for her. At 11 pm Stride was seen leaving the Bricklayers Arms pub on the Commercial Road together with a man who was kissing and cuddling her. He was described as being short with a dark moustache and wearing a morning suit and coat. She was next seen at about 11.45 pm in Berner Street standing in a doorway talking to a man in a short black cutaway coat and a sailor's hat. Both these men were presumed by police to have been clients.

At a little after half past midnight she was seen again in Berner Street, this time by PC William Smith, who noticed her talking to yet another man. This client was described by Smith as being about 28 years old, wearing a dark coat and a hard deerstalker hat and carrying a parcel wrapped in newspaper that was about six inches high and 18 inches in length.

Two other witnesses claimed to have seen Stride after PC Smith. James Brown was walking along Fairclough Street (at the end of Berner Street) when he saw Stride with a man about 5 feet 7 inches tall in a long black coat. Brown heard Stride say: 'No, not tonight, some other night.' Brown was not entirely certain of the time, but thought it may have been about 12.45 am. At about the same time, though again not certain, Israel Schwartz was walking along Berner Street. He saw a woman having an argument with a man. Schwartz later identified Stride's body as being that of the woman he saw. He said the man was about 30 years old, 5 feet 5 inches tall with dark hair and a small brown moustache. He was dressed in an overcoat and an old black felt hat with a wide brim. The man pushed the woman, who fell over.

At this point a second man standing nearby shouted 'Lipski' (the name of a man who had murdered his wife in Whitechapel in 1887). Suddenly worried he might be walking into trouble, Schwartz turned and hurried away back to Commercial Road. The second man followed him a short distance, then stopped. For some reason the police did not take Schwartz's evidence very seriously and he was not called to the inquest a few days later.

HAD CATHERINE EDDOWES BEEN SEEN WITH THE RIPPER?

The City Police were meanwhile struggling to identify the horribly mutilated corpse found on their patch in Mitre Square. The body had been ripped apart, and unlike earlier killings the face had also been mutilated. This made the usual mortuary photo almost useless as a means of establishing identification. However in a pocket had been found two pawn tickets, one for a man's shirt in the name of Emily Birrell, the other for a pair of men's boots in the name of Anne Kelly. The pawnbrokers were able to identify the tickets, but could not remember anything about the women they had served. In the hopes that the names might mean something to somebody, the police released the names and types of items pawned to the press.

On 2 October a man named John Kelly called at Bishopsgate Police Station and said that he thought he knew who the victim might be. He was taken to the mortuary and identified the body as that of his girlfriend Catherine Conway. His story was that he and Catherine had gone hop-picking in Kent. While there they had met a couple named Birrell, and Emily Birrell had given Catherine a pawn ticket for a shirt that might fit Kelly. He and Catherine had returned to London on 28 September when Catherine had pawned his spare boots for half a crown, which they used to buy food. At 2 pm Catherine had parted from Kelly saying that she was going to Bermondsey to see her adult daughter to see if she could borrow any money. She promised to return, but she did not. He then went back to Cooney's Lodging House, 55 Flower and Dean Street, where he and Catherine had usually stayed. She did not turn up there either, but when he read about the two pawn tickets he at once guessed that she was the latest murder victim.

Armed with the name of Catherine Conway and Kelly's knowledge that she was the widow of a retired soldier and had originally come from Wolverhampton, the police went to work to track her life story in case there was a reason for her murder. They discovered that she had been born in 1842 as Catherine Eddowes and brought up by an aunt after her mother died. At the age of 21 she ran off with a retired soldier named Thomas Conway. The pair lived off Conway's pension and from selling books and printed ballads, many of them topical rhymes written by Conway. They lived together until 1881, when they split. It was then that Conway had moved to Cooney's and had met Kelly. Although she called herself Catherine Conway there is no evidence she had ever married Conway, so her name is usually given as Catherine Eddowes.

The police also managed to track her movements on the day she was killed. After leaving Kelly she did not go to Bermondsey, but instead went to a pub and began drinking heavily. At 8 pm she was found drunk in Aldgate High Street by PC Louis Robinson. Robinson reckoned she was incapable of looking after herself, so he took her to Bishopsgate Police Station where she was put in the cells to sober up.

By 1 am Sergeant Byfield believed she was sober enough to find her way home and let her go. Before she left, she had a short conversation with PC Hutt.

'What time is it?' she asked Hutt.

'Too late for you to get anything to drink,' he replied.

'I shall get a damn fine hiding when I get home,' she said.

'And serve you right, you had no right to get drunk,' came the reply from Hutt as he opened the front door. 'This way, missus.'

'All right,' were her parting words. 'Goodnight, old cock.' Hutt watched her walk off steadily enough towards Aldgate High Street.

At 1.35 am Joseph Lawende, a commercial traveller in the cigarette trade, left the Imperial Club in Duke Street along with his friends Joseph Hyam Levy and Harry Harris. As they walked along Duke Street Levy pointed to a couple standing on the corner of Church Passage which led to Mitre Square. He said: 'Look there, I don't like going home by myself when I see those characters about.'

His two companions then looked across the road and saw a woman that they later identified as Eddowes talking to a man. Lawende described the man as 30 years old, 5 feet 7 inches tall, fair complexion and moustache with a medium build. He was wearing a pepper and salt coloured jacket which fitted loosely, a grey cloth cap with a peak of the same colour and had a reddish handkerchief knotted around his neck.

Given that the body of Eddowes was found only ten minutes later, the police quickly came to the conclusion that the man seen by Lawende, Levy and Harris was the killer. Lawende, who had taken more notice of the man than the other two, was taken into police custody for detailed questioning.

While the police were going through the motions of identifying the victims and fruitlessly searching in their pasts for a reason for murder, events on the streets were moving at some speed.

ARRESTED FOR HAVING CLEAN BOOTS

A policeman on patrol near Mitre Square on the Sunday evening spotted a man acting suspiciously and questioned him. The man was seen to have a brightly coloured scarf around his neck on which were several long hairs, obviously from a woman. The man said he had just arrived in London, having walked from Southampton. The policeman noticed, however, that his boots were clean instead of being road-stained so he arrested the man. Less than an hour later another arrest was made, this time of a man who was behaving in what was described as 'a very excitable fashion' near the murder scene in Berner Street. At 3 am a third arrest followed when a prostitute pointed out to a constable a man who had robbed her at knifepoint earlier in the night. Investigations found that all three could account for their movements on the night of the double murder and they were let go, apart from the third who was charged with robbery.

At 11 am on 2 October a woman named Amy Delling was walking down Chambers Street when a man approached her and made some lewd remarks about her attractive appearance. Being a respectable, if poor woman, Delling screamed for help, summoning the local beat policeman. By this time a crowd had gathered. Its members quickly became convinced that the man was the murderer and they turned violent. The policeman arrested the man for his own safety and with some difficulty got him safely to Leman Street Police Station. It turned out that the man was a slightly drunk sailor looking for a prostitute. After being charged and fined for being drunk and disorderly he was let go.

Later that day a knife with a 12-inch blade was found in Long Acre. It was pointed out to a policeman who took it away for study, but it was soon found it was the wrong shape to have inflicted the injuries.

ANGER TOWARDS THE POLICE

Another crowd gathered in Berner Street, and its mood also was ugly. This time it was the police who were the targets of the anger. The crowd ebbed and flowed as people came and went, but everyone was agreed that the police should have caught the killer and had failed to do so only because the victims were poor East Enders, not respectable women from a better area of London. Perhaps in response to this feeling, which was widespread in poorer areas of London, the City Police issued the following statement:

MURDER – £500 REWARD

Whereas, at 1.45. a.m., on Sunday, the 30th of September last, a woman, name unknown, was found brutally murdered in Mitre square, Aldgate, in this City, a Reward of £500 will be paid by the

Commissioner of Police of the City of London to any person (other than a person belonging to a Police Force in the United Kingdom) who shall give such information as shall lead to the discovery and conviction of the Murderer or Murderers. Information to be given to the Inspector of the Detective Department, 25 Old Jewry, or at any Police Station.

JAMES FRASER (Colonel), Commissioner.

The City Corporation announced that they were adding £200, the Stock Exchange put in £300, the Lord Mayor £50 and the London newspapers between them another £500. There was now ample incentive for anyone with even the slightest bit of evidence to come forward. Nobody did.

LETTERS FROM THE KILLER

Meanwhile, Inspector Reid had remembered something. On 27 September Scotland Yard had received a letter from a man claiming to be the killer. One element of it tied in to the post-mortem of Catherine Eddowes. Among the various mutilations to the dead woman's face was that her left earlobe had been cut off and could not be found.

The letter had read:

Dear Boss,

I keep on hearing the police have caught me but they wont fix me just yet. I have laughed when they look so clever and talk about being on the right track. That joke about Leather Apron gave me real fits. I am down on whores and I shant quit ripping them till I do get buckled. Grand work the last job was. I gave the lady no time to squeal. How can they catch me now. I love my work and want to start again. You will soon hear of me with my funny little games. I *saved some of the proper <u>red</u> stuff in a ginger beer bottle over the last job to write with but it went thick like glue and I cant use it. Red ink is fit enough I hope <u>ha. ha</u>. The next job I do I shall clip the ladys ears off and send to the police officers just for jolly wouldn't you. Keep this letter back till I do a bit more work, then give it out straight. My knife's so nice and sharp I want to get to work right away if I get a chance. Good Luck. Yours truly*

Jack the Ripper

Dont mind me giving the trade name

PS Wasnt good enough to post this before I got all the red ink off my hands curse it No luck yet. They say I'm a doctor now. <u>ha ha</u>

On 1 October the police received a postcard, obviously written by the same man, which read:

I was not codding dear old Boss when I gave you the tip, you'll hear about Saucy Jacky's work tomorrow double event this time number one squealed a bit couldn't finish straight off. Had not got time to get ears off for police thanks for keeping last letter back till I got to work again.

Jack the Ripper

At first the police were inclined to believe the letters were genuine. The first letter had mentioned, some days before the attack took place, that the killer would 'clip the ladys ears off', while the second mentioned the double killing before details were known to the public. Facsimiles of the two letters were printed and widely circulated in the hope that someone would recognize the handwriting. The only discernible effect, however,

The 'Dear Boss' letter introduced the name of Jack the Ripper to the public. The killer has been known by this name ever since.

was that the killer, previously dubbed 'Leather Apron' or 'Whitechapel Killer' now had a new and much more evocative name – 'Jack the Ripper'.

The police later changed their minds about these two letters. The handwriting was quite unlike that of the Goulston Street chalk writing while the time of the postmark on the second note was after the police had released details to press reporters. It became clear that the letters were the work of a journalist, and they were discounted by the police. Dozens of other letters, all signed Jack the Ripper, were then sent to the police and the newspapers, all written in different hands and presumably all the work of hoaxers.

The inquests into the two murders had meanwhile taken place and had been reported in exhaustive detail by the London newspapers, and in rather less detail by newspapers across Britain. The first sensation at the inquest into Elizabeth Stride came when the coroner ruled that the body might not be that of Stride since it had also been identified as being that of Elizabeth Watts. Mrs Watts' sister, Mary Malcolm, gave evidence that the body was her sister – from whom she was estranged – then added the following:

> I was in bed, and about twenty minutes past one on Sunday morning I felt a pressure on my breast and heard three distinct kisses. It was that which made me afterwards suspect that the woman who had been murdered was my sister.

The arrival of evidence of the supernatural caused a sensation and was splashed across newspapers the length and breadth of Britain – and abroad. All of which came as a great annoyance to Elizabeth Watts who wanted nothing more to do with her sister or with London. She got on a train, presented herself at the coroner's inquest next day and demanded to be allowed to give evidence that she was, in fact, still alive. She was first up and in evidence that caused great amusement in the newspapers declared:

> I want to clear my character. My sister I have not seen for years. She has given me a dreadful character. Her evidence is all false. This has put me to a dreadful trouble and trial. I have only a poor crippled husband, who is now outside. It is a shame my sister should say what she has said about me, and that the innocent should suffer for the guilty.

After the sensation of the doctor at Annie Chapman's inquest refusing to give his full findings, the public was agog to learn what the doctors would say this time. At the inquest into Elizabeth Stride, Dr George Phillips gave evidence in full. The death had been caused by the cutting of the artery in the neck and, given the size of the cut, would have been very quick. He was convinced from the splash pattern of blood at the scene that the woman had been lying where she was found when her throat had been cut – as had been the case in the previous murders.

It was, however, at the inquest into Catherine Eddowes where sensation was expected for it had been her body that the press had reported as being mutilated. Dr Frederick Brown gave his evidence on 4 October to a packed courtroom. Outside waited a host of telegram boys ready to take reports from the journalists inside. Dr Brown did not disappoint.

THE SCALE OF THE MUTILATIONS IS REVEALED

After detailing that death was caused by cutting of the throat and that this had been done when the victim was already lying on the ground, Dr Brown was asked by Coroner S.F. Langham: 'There were other wounds on the lower part of the body?' Brown proceeded to give a detailed account of what he found that brought gasps and cries from the public gallery, with one woman hurrying out apparently about to be sick. If this was what the earlier inquest had left unsaid, the public now knew what Jack the Ripper was up to.

The face was very much mutilated. There was a cut about a quarter of an inch through the lower left eyelid, dividing the structures completely through. The upper eyelid on that side, there was a scratch through the skin on the left upper eyelid, near to the angle of the nose. The right eyelid was cut through to about half an inch.

There was a deep cut over the bridge of the nose, extending from the left border of the nasal bone down near the angle of the jaw on the right side of the cheek. This cut went into the bone and divided all the structures of the cheek except the mucous membrane of the mouth.

The tip of the nose was quite detached by an oblique cut from the bottom of the nasal bone to where the wings of the nose join on to the face. A cut from this divided the upper lip and extended through the substance of the gum over the right upper lateral incisor tooth.

About half an inch from the top of the nose was another oblique cut. There was a cut on the right angle of the mouth as if the cut of a point of a knife. The cut extended an inch and a half, parallel with the lower lip.

There was on each side of cheek a cut which peeled up the skin, forming a triangular flap about an inch and a half. On the left cheek there were two abrasions of the epithelium under the left ear.

We examined the abdomen. The front walls were laid open from the breast bones to the pubes. The cut commenced opposite the enciform cartilage. The incision went upwards, not penetrating the skin that was over the sternum. It then divided the enciform cartilage. The knife must have cut obliquely at the expense of that cartilage.

Behind this, the liver was stabbed as if by the point of a sharp instrument. Below this was another incision into the liver of about two and a half inches, and below this the left lobe of the liver was slit through by a vertical cut. Two cuts were shewn by a jagging of the skin on the left side.

The abdominal walls were divided in the middle line to within a quarter of an inch of the navel. The cut then took a horizontal course for two inches and a half towards the right side. It then divided round the navel on the left side, and made a parallel incision to the former horizontal incision, leaving the navel on a tongue of skin. Attached to the navel was two and a half inches of the lower part of the rectus muscle on the left side of the abdomen.

The incision then took an oblique direction to the right and was shelving. The incision went down the right side of the vagina and rectum for half an inch behind the rectum.

There was a stab of about an inch on the left groin. This was done by a pointed instrument. Below this was a cut of three inches going through all tissues making a wound of the peritoneum about the same extent. An inch below the crease of the thigh was a cut extending from the anterior spine of the ilium obliquely down the inner side of the left thigh and separating the left labium, forming a flap of skin up to the groin. The left rectus muscle was not detached.

There was a flap of skin formed by the right thigh, attaching the right labium, and extending up to the spine of the ilium. The muscles on the right side inserted into the frontal ligaments were cut through.

The skin was retracted through the whole of the cut through the abdomen, but the vessels were not clotted. Nor had there been any appreciable bleeding from the vessels. I draw the conclusion that the act was made after death, and there would not have been much blood on the murderer. The cut was made by someone on the right side of the body, kneeling below the middle of the body.

The intestines had been detached to a large extent from the mesentery. About two feet of the colon was cut away. The sigmoid flexure was invaginated into the rectum very tightly. Right kidney was pale, bloodless with slight congestion of the base of the pyramids.

There was a cut from the upper part of the slit on the under surface of the liver to the left side, and another cut at right angles to this, which were about an inch and a half deep and two and a half inches long. Liver itself was healthy.

The gall bladder contained bile. The pancreas was cut, but not through, on the left side of the spinal column. Three and a half inches of the lower border of the spleen by half an inch was attached only to the peritoneum.

The peritoneal lining was cut through on the left side and the left kidney carefully taken out and removed. The left renal artery was cut through. I would say that someone who knew the position of the kidney must have done it. The lining membrane over the uterus was cut through. The womb was cut through horizontally, leaving a stump of three quarters of an inch. The rest of the womb had been taken away with some of the ligaments. The vagina and cervix of the womb was uninjured.

The bladder was healthy and uninjured, and contained three or four ounces of water. There was a tongue-like cut through the anterior wall of the abdominal aorta. The other organs were healthy. There were no indications of connexion. The wounds on the face and abdomen prove that they were inflicted by a sharp, pointed knife, and that in the abdomen by one six inches or longer.

I believe the perpetrator of the act must have had considerable knowledge of the position of the organs in the abdominal cavity and the way of removing them. It required a great deal of medical knowledge to have removed the kidney and to know where it was placed. The parts removed would be of no use for any professional purpose.

I think the perpetrator of this act had sufficient time, or he would not have nicked the lower eyelids. It would take at least five minutes.

It was horrific stuff. Not every newspaper printed the details of the injuries. The *Daily Telegraph*, for instance, missed out nearly all of Dr Brown's testimony and inserted instead the words 'Witness here described in detail the terrible mutilation of the deceased's body'. The *East London Advertiser* summarized his evidence in just six lines. The *Evening News*, by contrast, printed the evidence in full.

London, and the East End in particular, was now very much aware of the horror in its midst. And still neither the police nor the vigilants could catch Jack the Ripper.

CHAPTER 8:

THE MISSING KIDNEY

The murders had reached what seemed to be a peak of horror with two killings in one night, but things were only going to get worse. A few days later George Lusk opened a box he received in the post. Inside was a human kidney that matched the one missing from the body of Catherine Eddowes, along with a note saying the killer had eaten part of the body. The revelations plunged London into a state of fear. But then a piece of grotesque light relief came to the fore.

THE MANHUNT GAINS SOME ODD RECRUITS

On the night of 5 October PC Mackenzie was on fixed point duty (meaning he stayed in one place instead of walking a beat) in Heath Street, Hampstead, when he became aware of a fracas outside the Horse and Groom pub some yards away in Hampstead High Street. Mackenzie went to investigate and found a woman dancing about while a group of men shouted insults at her. When the policeman came into view, the men fell silent, but the woman continued to prance about. Thinking that there was something odd about the woman, but not sure quite what, Mackenzie told her to be on her way. The woman then produced a knife, whereupon Mackenzie wrestled her to the ground and disarmed her. It was at this point that Mackenzie realized the woman was, in fact, a man wearing a dress, bonnet and jacket. He arrested the man and took him to the police station.

The case was heard at Hampstead Magistrates' Court next morning. The man identified himself as William Webb, a labourer. He said he had been drinking with friends when they had goaded him about not having enough courage to go to Whitechapel and track down Jack the Ripper. Webb had then gone home, changed into some clothes of his wife's and gone back to the pub saying that he would go to Whitechapel, pretend to be a prostitute and so trap the killer. He had been giving his impression of how a prostitute walked down the street looking for clients when PC Mackenzie had turned up. He was fined ten shillings for being drunk and disorderly.

Webb was not the only man to have the same idea, nor the only one to come to grief. On the night of 8 October a reporter from the *East London Advertiser* dressed as a woman and set out to try to entice Jack the Ripper into making a move. He got only as far as Borough Market before a woman called out, 'Hey. Here's a man dressed as a woman!' That brought a crowd to the scene, which the reporter could not shake off. He instead went home in some disgrace.

The following day a spiritualist came forward to tell police that her spirit guide had revealed to her a vision of the killer. He was, she declared,

of the appearance of a farmer, but dressed like a navvy with a strap round his waist and peculiar pockets. He had a dark moustache and scars behind his ears, besides other marks. He will commit one more murder and be caught red-handed.

The police thanked the spiritualist, then sent her away again.

Meanwhile a letter was received by the *East London Observer* addressed to the Joseph Lawende who had seen Catherine Eddowes with the man assumed to have been her killer. It read:

You thought your-self very clever I reckon when you informed the
police. But you made a mistake if you thought I dident see you.
Now I known you know me and I see your little game, and I mean
to finish you and send your ears to your wife if you show this to the
police or help them if you do I will finish you. It no use your trying
to get out of my way. Because I have you when you dont expect it
and I keep my word as you soon see and rip you up.

Yours truly Jack the Ripper.

Again the letter was at first thought to be genuine, but was later to be
dismissed as a fake.

VIGILANCE COMMITTEE AND POLICE JOIN FORCES

Of rather more use to the police were the men of the Whitechapel
Vigilance Committee. The two bodies were now working closely together.
The police had given George Lusk, the chairman of the committee, the
details of the beats their men were patrolling, on condition he kept them
secret, and he set his men to patrol intersecting routes so that every street
and court was visited as often as possible. The co-operation did not
always work as well as might be hoped. On the evening of 6 October
one plainclothes detective went to Whitechapel to follow up a lead. He
quickly found himself being covertly followed by a tough man armed
with a large wooden club – who turned out to be one of Mr Lusk's men
who thought the detective was acting suspiciously.

Such mishaps aside, the Vigilance Committee had been using their
local contacts to try to produce clues and so help the police. By early
October they had come to the conclusion (by means that they did not
make public) that the killer was a local man who had been living in
Whitechapel for at least some years, possibly his entire life. Moreover

they thought that he probably lived in the maze of narrow streets that extended between Whitechapel High Street in the south to the railway lines out of Liverpool Street Station in the north, and from Middlesex Street in the west to Brick Lane in the east. They began to concentrate their efforts there.

Sir Charles Warren had decided that no expense should be spared in finding the killer. He therefore took up one of the most modern aids known to detective work: bloodhounds. A number of these dogs specially trained to follow scents were brought to London. Warren gave strict instructions that should another body be found it had to be left untouched until the dogs could be fetched and used to follow the scent of the killer.

FEAR AND RUMOURS SPAN BRITAIN

On 11 October news spread rapidly through east London that a new body had been discovered in Arbour Street, just off Commercial Road in Whitechapel. By 11 am a crowd had gathered in the narrow street, but nobody could discover anything definite. At 11.15 am a policeman arrived, called for silence and announced that no murdered woman had been found. It was simply a false rumour.

Barely had that event died down than fresh word ran around that a dead body had been found in Hanbury Street, scene of the murder of Annie Chapman. This time there was some truth in the rumour. Mrs Sodeaux of 65 Hanbury Street had been getting increasingly depressed over recent weeks and had become obsessed with the idea that the killer would strike her next. She had left her 8-year-old child saying she was popping to a shop, but when she did not come back the child tried to find her. The woman was found hanging by the neck from the banister on the top floor of the house. She had clearly committed suicide.

The excitement and terror had by this date reached far beyond London. On 12 October an elderly woman was sitting on a park bench in Sheil Park, Liverpool, when she was approached by a man she described as being aged around 50 and respectably dressed. The man asked her if she knew where he could find some prostitutes. The woman was understandably surprised and at once stood up to walk off. The man asked her again, but she pushed past and made off as fast as she could. As she left the man shouted after her, 'I will kill as many women in Liverpool as I did in London!' The Liverpool police concluded that Jack the Ripper was in Liverpool, perhaps trying to board a ship to take him out of the country. They set men to watch any ship taking on passengers, but nobody answering the old woman's description was caught.

Soon afterwards the *Belfast Telegraph* received a letter signed 'Jack the Ripper' and written in red ink, presumably in imitation of blood. It read:

> Dear Boss, –*I have arrived in your city, as London is too warm for me just now, so that Belfast — had better look out, for I intend to commence operations on Saturday night. I have spotted some nice fat ones who will cut up well. I am longing to begin, for I love my work. –Yours, &c., JACK THE RIPPER.*

It was presumed to be a hoax, and no murders followed.

On 13 October the killings appeared to have taken a new turn of horror. A reporter at the London Hospital in Whitechapel saw a man with horrific wounds to his abdomen being carried in by police. Assuming Jack the Ripper had taken to attacking men, the reporter dashed off a news piece that he sent hotfoot to be published. It later turned out that the man was a butcher who had accidentally stabbed himself when jointing up a quarter of beef.

The same day George Lusk received a letter with a Kilburn postmark that he took to the police. It seemed to be in the same handwriting as the earlier letter, starting 'Dear Boss', and it was written in black ink. It read:

I write you a letter in black ink, as I have no more of the right stuff.
I think you are all asleep in Scotland-yard with your bloodhounds,
as I will show you to-morrow night. I am going to do a double event,
but not in Whitechapel. Got rather too warm there. Had to shift. No
more till you hear me again. JACK THE RIPPER.

The police told him to ignore it, though they did not explain that they were certain the writer was a London journalist.

The earlier letters turned up a clue that, it was hoped, might lead to a swift arrest. Facsimiles of the Dear Boss letter had been circulated throughout Britain, not just in London. On 13 October a shipping clerk in Newcastle upon Tyne was going through the paperwork lodged by a ship that had just left for France, having arrived in Newcastle from Faversham in Kent. The signature of one of the sailors looked to him to be identical to that of Jack the Ripper on the Dear Boss letter. An urgent telegram was sent to Scotland Yard, who promptly sent word on to France that the man was to be arrested on arrival and held for questioning. A policeman left for France to conduct the questioning. It transpired the sailor had been out of the country on other ships at the time of two of the murders, and so was dropped as a suspect. Given that the Dear Boss letter was now considered a hoax this cannot have come as much of a surprise.

FREE PARDON OFFERED TO INFORMANTS

George Lusk also got another letter from the Home Secretary. Having had their idea of a large reward turned down by the government, the

Whitechapel Vigilance Committee had come up with another idea. They speculated that the killer might be part of a criminal gang. The members of that gang might have their suspicions about their colleague's behaviour but were reluctant to go to the police for fear that they might be arrested for whatever crimes they had committed as a gang. The committee had therefore written to the Home Secretary suggesting that anyone who gave evidence leading to a conviction should be given a free pardon for their own crimes.

This time the Home Secretary was more open to the idea. He responded that he would be willing to offer a free pardon to anyone coming forward with information, but only if that pardon did not include acts related to the murders themselves. The offer was made public in the newspapers on 15 October.

In the same edition of the *Evening News* as the offer of a free pardon, there was a theory by a 'Medical Man', who speculated as to the motives of the murders. After discussing and rejecting various ideas the writer of the article stated:

> *There can, however, be little doubt that in the Whitechapel atrocities we are brought face to face with all the evidences of what is termed 'Lustmord,' i.e., murder (and mutilation too) committed from purely voluptuous motives, the perpetrator being one of those strange individuals who are otherwise unable to obtain complete sexual gratification. This peculiar form of psycho-pathy is termed 'Perversion of the sexual impulse' (*Perversion des Geschlichtstriebes*) by von Krafft-Ebing, who, in his interesting and instructive work, entitled 'Psychopathia Sexualis,' distinctly states that in all cases of murder with mutilation, in which the bowels and genital organs have been either simply excised, or carried away as well, it may confidently be assumed that a 'Lustmord' has been committed.*

A HUMAN KIDNEY ARRIVES IN THE POST

The day after this article appeared, George Lusk received a packet in the post measuring about three inches square. Inside was a kidney which had been preserved in red wine and a letter which read:

From hell.

Mr Lusk,

Sor

I send you half the Kidne I took from one woman and prasarved it for you tother piece I fried and ate it was very nise. I may send you the bloody knif that took it out if you only wate a whil longer

signed

Catch me when you can Mishter Lusk

Having been told by police to ignore the previous letter he had received, Lusk was inclined to ignore this one as well. However his colleague on the Vigilance Committee, Aarons, persuaded him to have the kidney checked to see if it was human or animal. He therefore took it to his doctor, Dr Frederick Wiles of Mile End Road. Wiles passed it on to Thomas Openshaw, the head of pathology at the nearby London Hospital. Openshaw quickly recognized the kidney as being a human left kidney of about the size and characteristics that would match the right kidney left in the body of Catherine Eddowes. There was, however, no way to test if it had actually come from Eddowes.

The letter therefore took on new importance and was taken to the police. They recognized that the poor spelling was similar to that of the chalk writing found in Goulston Street. The police were not sure whether they should credit the letter as being genuine or not. It was not unknown for medical students to take organs from bodies to play macabre tricks on each other, and this kidney might have been one such.

THE BLOODY LODGER OF BATTY STREET

On 16 October the press got hold of some information that the police had been keeping private for more than two weeks. In the early hours of 30 September, less than an hour after the double murders of that night, the landlady of an unidentified guest house had been woken up when one of her lodgers came home more noisily than usual. The next morning he had announced that he was going away for a couple of weeks, but would be back and asked Mrs Kuer both to store a bag for him and to keep the room. He paid his bills and left. The landlady was revealed some days later to be Mrs Kuer of 22 Batty Street, but this was as yet still kept secret.

A couple of days after the man had left, Mrs Kuer opened the bag he had given her. It contained clothes, including a shirt that was heavily bloodstained around the cuffs and lower arms. Horrified by the link between a bloody shirt and the date her lodger had left, she told her neighbours then went to the police. They took the news seriously enough to station two men permanently inside 22 Batty Street so that they would be on hand to arrest the missing lodger when he returned, an event expected on Saturday 13 October. The Saturday came and went, and no lodger returned. The police, it was reported on 16 October, were still watching the house and were following other lines of investigation about the missing lodger.

It all sounded very promising, but the story soon began to unravel. Mrs Kuer began by speaking to reporters about her mysterious missing lodger, then announced that the matter had all been cleared up and refused to speak to the press. The police were no less obscure. They began by denying the story completely, then said that the story was true but that the lodger had been traced and questioned with the result that he had been eliminated from inquiries. The story then changed to say that the bloody shirt had been left not by a lodger but by a neighbour for whom Mrs Kuer did the laundry.

On 17 October a lodger at the house wrote a letter that he sent to the London newspapers. It ran:

SIR – The police are not in the house, nor has the woman had a lodger who is now missing, but a stranger brought the shirts, and when he fetched them, he was detained by the police, and after inquiries discharged. As regards our house, it is not as your report describes it, for it is a most respectable house and in good general condition; although it is certainly not Windsor Castle. There are only two lodgers, one a drayman, name of Joseph, who works for the Norwegian Lager Beer Company, and the other a baker, name of Carl Noun, who has been at work in Margate, and only returned on the 6th of this month after the season was over. I trust you will publish these statements as I put it to you, in fact it may injure the poor woman in her business. – Respectfully.

C. NOUN (a lodger in the house). 22, Batty-street, Commercial-road, E., October 17.

Thereafter the story of the Bloody Lodger of Batty Street faded away from the public gaze. There was, after all, plenty to keep the East End of London on its toes. There was, for instance, the unfortunate woman who was found gibbering with fright on a tram in Whitechapel. The conductor could get no sense out of her, other than the fact that she was being chased by a murderer, so he called the police. The woman turned out to be Mrs Sarah Goody of Stepney, a seamstress who worked at home. Her landlady said that she had been behaving oddly recently, claiming that men were following her and that men had been writing messages to her on the house windows. She was taken to the workhouse infirmary, and very quickly the staff there concluded that she was insane, having been driven mad by the terror induced by Jack the Ripper.

The police had meanwhile been searching every house, lodging house, tenement and other dwelling in the area between Brick Lane and Middlesex Street where it was thought the murderer might be living. The police had handed out handbills to every resident explaining what they were looking for and why, and had searched the properties thoroughly. The task had taken several days to complete, but nothing had been found.

At 1 am on 18 October a woman was found lying on the pavement in Bermondsey with blood pouring across her throat and over her clothes. The policeman who found her feared that her throat was cut and that the Whitechapel killer had moved to start killing south of the River Thames. He summoned assistance and soon the news was spreading through south London. Once the woman was at a hospital, however, it turned out the blood had come from a deep cut on her chin. She had obviously drunk herself almost insensible and was presumed to have fallen over in the street and cut herself.

FALSE LEADS, FALSE HOPES

The arrests continued to be made. On 19 October a man was arrested in Bermondsey after a pair of local men pointed him out to police as having acted strangely. He turned out to be an American new to London who had lost his way. Three days later a woman was arrested and charged with wasting police time for having written a number of letters that she signed 'Jack the Ripper' and then sent to newspapers. On 23 October a man was arrested near Bow Church after he was seen washing blood from his waistcoat, but he was let go after giving the police a satisfactory explanation. The following night a man was arrested in Whitechapel Road after pestering a woman outside a pub. The newspapers leapt on the story, but in the event he was charged only with being drunk and disorderly.

Perhaps more constructive was the opening on 18 October of a cheap boarding house for women only – the first of its kind in Whitechapel – in Mile End Road. It was intended for the use of women of good character who were impoverished and without the support or company of a man. It soon filled up, proving if nothing else that some women did not want to share sleeping quarters with men they did not know as they had to do in common lodging houses. A few days later the Ratcliff Highway Refuge and Night Shelter was opened. This institution aimed at helping destitute teenage girls to learn a decent trade before they became old enough to fall into prostitution.

Police and others had by this date noticed an apparent pattern in the murders. Martha Tabram had been killed on 7 August, Mary Nichols on 31 August, Annie Chapman on 8 September and Stride and Eddowes on 30 September. Each killing had taken place at the weekend, or on a bank holiday Monday. If the pattern had been followed there should have been a murder on about 7 or 8 October, but there had been none.

As 30 October approached tension rose again as it was assumed a murder would take place then or on the following weekend. The newspapers began to report on the apparent pattern to the dates and speculated that a murder was imminent. On 28 October chalk writing on a wall in Deptford was found that read, 'I shall do another murder and will receive her heart'.

Fruit salesman Matthew Packer, who claimed to have sold a bunch of grapes to Stride and a suspicious man the night she was murdered, announced he had seen the man again.

I was standing with my barrow at the corner of Greenfield-street, Commercial-road, when I saw a man pass by on the opposite side of Greenfield-street, near the watchmaker's shop. I recognized him in a minute as the man I had seen outside my shop on the night when Elizabeth Stride was murdered in Berner-street. It was the man who bought the grapes and gave them to the woman that was afterwards found murdered in the yard. I shall never forget his face, and should know him again amongst a thousand men. I was pretty right knocked over with fright. It gave me such a turn as I have never had in my life. I was too frightened and staggered to know what I was about, and I saw in a minute that the man knew me as well. He looked hard at me as he passed, with a most vicious look on his face, that made me think I should not have liked to have been with him in any quiet corner. I'm sure he'd have killed me. There were no policemen in sight, so I sent a young chap for a policeman, and the man seeing there was something up jumped into a tram that was going to Blackwall.

If Packer was to be believed, the killer was still at large and walking Whitechapel.

There was almost a riot in Camden Town on the evening of 29 October when a man rushed up to some women outside a pub in Bayham Street and made lewd suggestions to them. When some men appeared to defend the women the man pulled a knife and shouted, 'Get back, get back. I am Jack the Ripper.' At this point the men rushed him and began to beat him. The man was rescued by a policeman who dragged him to the police station. Within half an hour a crowd estimated to be 1,000 strong demanded that the man be handed over to them. The police called for reinforcements, and announced to the crowd that the man would appear in court at 9 am next morning. He was duly put up in front of Magistrate Bros at Clerkenwell Court. The man turned out to be a hairdresser named Frederick Dunbar. He was by this time suffering from a hangover and was in a sorry state. He apologized for what he had done, saying he could explain only that he had been drunk. Mr Bros eyed him coldly then announced: 'You have made a fool of yourself, and I will send you to prison for twenty-one days' imprisonment with hard labour. Take him down.'

Another man to feel the force of the law was 17-year-old George Randall who, on 30 October, put out a street light in Upper Thames Street, plunging a busy footpath near Cannon Street railway station into darkness. Local residents assumed the light had been put out by Jack the Ripper to allow him to pounce on passing women. Randall was arrested and fined ten shillings by the Lord Mayor of London who declared:

If persons like the defendant indulge in this kind of practical joking they must pay for it. The defendant had no doubt done it by way of a senseless joke, to create a panic in the neighbourhood, and he must be fined 10 shillings. If any more cases of the kind came before the Court the maximum penalty of 40 shillings will be imposed.

The forces of law and order were clearly taking no chances. And the dreaded weekend of 3 November passed without incident. Well, almost without incident. A policeman on patrol in Harrington Gardens, Kensington, saw a parcel apparently discarded into the front garden of a house. He found it was only loosely wrapped and contained two large and murderously sharp knives of a most peculiar design that had old dried bloodstains on them. The knives were taken back to the police station and there identified as kukri knives, the weapon used for hand-to-hand combat by Gurkha regiments in the Indian Army. The police denied that the weapons had any link to the Whitechapel murders, but some speculated that the killer had given up his rampage and had thrown away his weapons.

They were to be proved most cruelly wrong on the morning of 9 November.

CHAPTER 9:

THE KELLY KILLING

As the people of London saw horror piled upon horror, it must have seemed that nothing could be more terrible than the killings to date. But Jack the Ripper was by no means done yet. His next murder would be the most grotesque and horrific to date – so horrible that the police did not dare release the details to the public. Even today the gruesome details of the murder have the power to shock, while the mysteries surrounding the last hours of the victim have never been solved.

BARELY RECOGNIZABLE AS HUMAN

The news broke slowly on 9 November. When the *Evening News* went to press they could only report:

> *About noon today it was reported that another terrible murder like those which recently horrified the community had been perpetrated in Miller's court, Dorset street, Spitalfields. It will be remembered that the news of the other murders was very early made known, and consequently the late hour of the day in which the present intelligence came to us seemed to argue against the truth of the rumour. We at once sent a reporter to the spot, who, on applying to the inspector at the Commercial street Station, was informed that orders had been received not to give any information beyond the*

bare fact that a woman had been murdered, all official information being forwarded to Scotland yard. Consequently the details of the crime are difficult to obtain, but inquiry in the neighbourhood elicited the information that the victim's head was nearly, or quite severed from the body, and that, as in the other terrible cases, the abdomen was ripped open.

The same newspaper devoted much of its edition the next day to the horrific details of what had taken place in Dorset Street, but it also printed an editorial column as follows:

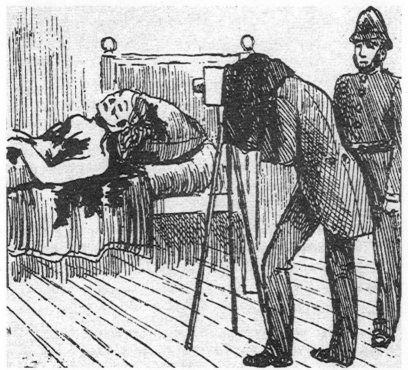

A contemporary sketch shows Kelly's body being photographed. The state of the body is only hinted at.

Again the East end fiend has been at work, and this time the insane love of mutilation is more apparent than ever. The victim in this case, Mary Ann [sic Jane] Kelly, has been cut, eviscerated, and disfigured as none of her unfortunate predecessors sacrificed by the 'Lust Morder' have been. Still the manner of the handicraft shows, we believe, that the same artist has been engaged. We call him an artist not in ridicule, but in very seriousness, from the evident fact that he loves his diabolical work, and endeavours to excite in ever increasing degree the attention of the world. His art is horror and he seeks ever to intensify it. On September 10 we ventured to suggest that the murderer was a monomaniac, and also possibly an epileptic. We did not then condemn the police, as many of our contemporaries did, for their failure to trace the assassin, recognising as we did the obscurity that surrounds the acts of the insane. Everything tends to the belief that one man and one man only is responsible for the series of murders, though fashion in murder as in suicide exerts potent influence on ill regulated minds. The atrocity of yesterday, a special and graphic account of which appears in other columns, shows, as in the other cases, that the murderer while revelling in mutilation is not a skilful anatomist. His knowledge, whatever it may be, is not that of a school bred man. He was proved in the Mitre square instance to have bungled his work, and if in the present case he has proceeded to greater lengths of horror, the more advantageous conditions of seclusion in a house amply explain it. Much was made by Sir Charles Warren of the use to which bloodhounds could be turned. Yesterday they were sent for, but they were not forthcoming. Perhaps there is no great loss in this. The proper bloodhounds in this matter must be the police, and in order to succeed in their search, they must abandon their time honoured traditions.

It was not only the London newspapers that covered the story. So famous had Jack the Ripper become that news of the latest murder spread across the world by telegraph to appear in numerous foreign newspapers. The *Atlanta Constitution* of Georgia in the USA devoted an entire page to the murder under the headline 'FIENDISH ATROCITY – The Details of Another Whitechapel Murder'.

Other American papers to give the story extensive coverage were the *Cincinnati Informer*, the *Boston Daily Globe* (headline 'Gory Tale of Whitechapel – Hacking Horrors Never Equalled'), the *New York Times*, the *New York Herald* and the *Bismarck Tribune* of North Dakota. The British Empire was also agog with newspapers in Sydney, Montreal, Manitoba, Auckland and Cape Town all devoting extensive coverage to the murder.

It was indeed a dramatic murder which, even if it had not been the work of Jack the Ripper, would have been worthy of extensive coverage.

It had been at about 10.30 am that John McCarthy sent his assistant Thomas Bowyer to collect overdue rent from a tenant named Mary Kelly. McCarthy was the landlord at Miller's Court (also known as McCarthy's Rents) in Dorset Street. The property consisted of a number of rooms which opened off a courtyard, linked to Dorset Street by a passageway. McCarthy lived and worked on site, having a chandler's shop on Dorset Street adjacent to the passage that led through a brick arch to the rooms he rented out. The passage led back for 20 feet before it opened out into a courtyard that contained a toilet, a water tap, a dustbin and a street lamp, lit at night. There were 13 rooms in all, arranged over two storeys, all of which opened on to the yard.

The tenant behind with her rent was Mary Jane Kelly (also known as Marie Jeanette Kelly), a prostitute living in Room No. 13. Those who knew her reckoned she was rather better than most prostitutes working in Whitechapel. She had her own room and so did not need to work on the streets. Moreover she was described as being attractive, pretty and personable. McCarthy was not in the habit of allowing tenants to get behind with their rent without evicting them and there were suggestions that he may have given Kelly some leeway in return for having enjoyed her favours. Be that as it may, on the morning of 9 November he wanted his money and sent Bowyer to get it.

Bowyer walked the few yards to Kelly's door and knocked. There was no reply, but he thought she was in as neither he nor McCarthy had seen her leave that morning. He therefore peered in through the window to No. 13 that overlooked the yard, and stepped back in horror. On the bed was a body so badly cut about and mutilated that it could barely be recognized as human, never mind identified as Kelly. He staggered back to McCarthy's office and gasped out the news. McCarthy dashed up the

A contemporary imagining of how the killer overpowered and murdered Mary Kelly.

passage to see for himself, then sent Bowyer running to get the police. Inspector Walter Dew later recounted what happened next.

If I remember rightly it was between ten and eleven o'clock in the morning that I looked in at Commercial Street police station to get in touch with my superiors. I was chatting with Inspector Beck, who was in charge of the station, when a young fellow, his eyes bulging out of his head, came panting into the police station. The poor fellow was so frightened that for a time he was unable to utter a single intelligible word. At last he managed to stammer out something about 'Another one. Jack the Ripper. Awful. Jack McCarthy sent me'. Mr McCarthy was well known to us as a common lodging house proprietor. 'Come along Dew', said Inspector Beck and gathering from the terrorized messenger that Dorset Street was the scene of whatever had happened, we made him our pilot, as we rushed in that direction, collecting as many constables as we could on the way.

Dew also peered through the window at the carnage within, as did Inspector Abberline and Dr George Phillips when they arrived at about 11.15 am. After waiting for two hours for Commissioner Warren and his bloodhounds to arrive, Superintendent Arnold decided to get on with it. He ordered McCarthy to smash the door open with an axe and decided that Phillips should be the first to enter. Phillips conducted a preliminary inspection of the body before it was taken away for an autopsy, which would be carried out by Dr Thomas Bond. Three photos of the crime scene were taken before the body was moved, making Mary Jane Kelly the only one of Jack the Ripper's victims to be photographed where she was found.

A POPULAR AND FRIENDLY VICTIM

Abberline then studied the room for clues, collecting everything present and recording where it had been. He noticed that a large fire had been burning in the grate the night before and that a quantity of women's clothing had been burned to ashes. The ashes were taken away to be carefully sifted for unburnt remnants. There was a clay pipe and a few other male odds and ends.

The first task for the police was to track Kelly's past to see if there was anyone who would have had a motive for murder. The killing might appear to be another by Jack the Ripper, but it was always possible that it had been made to look that way. McCarthy told the police that Kelly had arrived in Miller's Court in February 1888 along with a Billingsgate Market porter named Joseph Barnett. The couple were popular and friendly with the other residents. Kelly was not working as a prostitute at this time, the couple living off Barnett's wages. However, in September Barnett lost his job. Soon afterwards old prostitute friends of Kelly's began calling. Barnett objected to Kelly's friends, especially when one of them was allowed to stay overnight. He quarrelled with Kelly and moved out. Barnett had been back most days since to visit Kelly and sometimes gave her money. He had last called at 7.30 pm on 8 November, staying for about a quarter of an hour. One of the residents at Miller's Court told the police that there had been another man named Joe who had called on Kelly when Barnett was not there. He had been very friendly with Kelly and had given her money now and then.

Police quickly tracked down Barnett, who was living at 25 New Street, Bishopsgate. He was found to be a local man, who had been born in Whitechapel in 1858 and had lived there ever since. He told the police that he had met Kelly on Good Friday 1887 and within 48 hours they had decided to move in together, but not to marry. They lived in a succession of rented rooms around Whitechapel before moving to Miller's Court and had only once been in any sort of trouble – when they were evicted from rooms in Little Paternoster Row for not paying their rent. Barnett identified the pipe and other objects found in Kelly's room as being his.

Barnett said that Kelly had been born in Ireland in 1863 but that the family had moved to Wales when her father had got a job in the ironworks of Carmarthen when she was a toddler. Apparently the Kellys had been fairly well off, and Kelly had been better educated than most working class girls of her time. At the age of 16 Kelly married a local collier named Davis and had a baby. But Davis was killed in a mining accident two or three years later. For some reason Kelly did not go home to her family but instead moved to Cardiff where she became a prostitute. In about 1884 she moved to London where she worked in an upmarket brothel. She was so popular there with the wealthy gentleman clients that she would ride in their carriages and on at least one occasion went to Paris.

It was drink that was Kelly's downfall. She was abusive and aggressive when drunk, and she got so drunk so often when she was supposed to be sober that she was thrown out of the brothel. She then moved to a house in Breezer's Hill run by a Mrs Carthy. Although there was no real evidence to prove it, this seems to have been a less salubrious brothel. She left there in 1886 to live with a stonemason named Joseph Fleming. That relationship did not last long and she was living in a common lodging house in Thrawl Street when she met Barnett. Fleming was clearly the other Joe who had visited Kelly in Miller's Court. The police contacted Fleming and Mrs Carthy and, along with Barnett, ruled them out as suspects.

HAD MARY JANE KELLY'S KILLER BEEN SEEN?

Meanwhile, constables and detectives had been knocking on doors in the area looking for anyone who knew the victim. It was hoped that by retracing her movements on the night she was murdered they might find some clue to the killer. Until 8 pm on the night of her death Kelly had been in her room chatting to another resident of Miller's Court, Maria Harvey. At some point after that she went to the Ten Bells pub for a drink where she was seen with a woman who could not be identified. At 11 pm she was seen in the Britannia pub drinking with a man described as being young, smartly dressed and with a moustache. Kelly appeared to be drunk.

At 11.45 Mrs Mary Ann Cox was walking home to 5 Miller's Court. She entered Dorset Street from Commercial Street and saw Kelly with a man. She said the man was stout, aged around 35 and was about 5 feet 5 inches tall. He was dressed in a long overcoat and a dark hat. He had a blotchy face and small side whiskers and a carroty moustache. The man was carrying what looked like a pail of beer. Cox followed Kelly and the man she presumed to be a client into Miller's Court. She said goodnight as the couple were standing outside Kelly's room. A short time later Cox heard Kelly singing a favourite song of hers, 'A Violet from Mother's Grave'.

At 12.30 am Kelly's singing woke up Mr and Mrs Pickett, also residents in Miller's Court. Half an hour later Cox could still hear Kelly singing. At some point after 1 am Mrs Elizabeth Prater came home rather the worse for drink to the room she rented upstairs at 26 Dorset Street which overlooked Miller's Court. She could not hear any singing.

At 2 am a man named George Hutchinson, who already knew Kelly, was walking down Commercial Street. He met Kelly standing on the corner of Flower and Dean Street, some 50 yards south of Dorset Street. According to his later testimony, Kelly asked Hutchinson if he could lend her some money, but as he had no money on him Hutchinson refused. It has been suggested that in fact Kelly had tried to pick Hutchinson up as a client but he declined as he had no money. Hutchinson then watched as Kelly approached another man. He heard Kelly say, 'All right', and the man reply, 'You will be all right for what I have told you.'

Kelly and the man then headed down Dorset Street to Miller's Court. Hutchinson followed and saw the couple pause outside Miller's Court for a quick conversation, though all he heard was Kelly say, 'All right, my dear. Come along. You will be comfortable.' Hutchinson claimed that as Kelly and her client walked under a street light he got a good look at the man. He later described the man as having a pale complexion, a slight moustache turned up at the corners, dark hair, dark eyes and bushy eyebrows. He was wearing a soft felt hat pulled down over his eyes, a long dark coat trimmed in astrakhan, a white collar and a black tie fixed with a horseshoe pin. He wore dark spats with light buttons over button boots. A massive gold chain was in his waistcoat with a large seal with a red stone hanging from it. He carried kid gloves in his right hand and a small package in his left. He was about 5 feet 7 inches tall and about 35 or 36 years old.

At about 4 am Mrs Prater heard someone call softly, 'Oh, murder,' a call also heard by Sarah Lewis, another resident of Miller's Court. She ignored it as the cry was so common in the area and rarely meant more than that a fight had started. At 5.45 am Mrs Cox heard a man leave the court, but did not see him nor which room he left. None of the male inhabitants of the court later claimed to have been this man. At 7 am a flower girl who knew Kelly called to see if she could borrow one of Kelly's spare shawls as the weather was cold. She knocked on the door of No. 13, but got no answer.

Dr Bond later estimated the time of death to have been at between 3.30 am and 4.30 am. It was assumed therefore that the murder had taken place at 4 am and the killer had left at 5.45 am. Whether or not the man seen by Hutchinson was the murderer is unclear. He may have been, or he may have left after an hour or so with Kelly, who then went out to find another client.

The man seen with Kelly by George Hutchinson as drawn by a newspaper artist.

Once again the police were faced with a murder victim chosen apparently at random by a killer who murdered in silence and then melted away into Whitechapel as if he had never been there. It was all terribly frustrating.

THE WORLD'S FIRST CRIMINAL PROFILE

Back on 25 October Robert Anderson, head of the CID at Scotland Yard, decided to try a new approach to the killings. It proved to be an imaginative move that no police force had ever tried before, but which many would imitate in later years. He called in Dr Thomas Bond, the registered police surgeon for Westminster and a man with a reputation for an understanding of the human mind as much as of the human body. Anderson sent Bond the full notes of the autopsies and transcripts of the coroners' inquiries and asked him for his professional opinion. Bond replied on 10 November, producing what is considered to have been the world's first ever criminal profile. By the time he wrote the note he had had the chance to view the mutilated remains of Mary Kelly. After briefly reviewing the nature of the wounds inflicted by the killer, Bond continued:

> The mutilations in each case excepting the Berners Street one were all of the same character and shewed clearly that in all the murders, the object was mutilation.
>
> In each case the mutilation was inflicted by a person who had no scientific nor anatomical knowledge. In my opinion he does not even possess the technical knowledge of a butcher or horse slaughterer or any person accustomed to cut up dead animals.
>
> The instrument must have been a strong knife at least six inches long, very sharp, pointed at the top and about an inch in width. It

may have been a clasp knife, a butcher's knife or a surgeon's knife. I think it was no doubt a straight knife.

The murderer must have been a man of physical strength and of great coolness and daring. There is no evidence that he

Sir Robert Anderson, assistant commissioner at Scotland Yard at the time of the murders.

had an accomplice. He must in my opinion be a man subject to periodical attacks of Homicidal and erotic mania. The character of the mutilations indicate that the man may be in a condition sexually, that may be called satyriasis. It is of course possible that the Homicidal impulse may have developed from a revengeful or brooding condition of the mind, or that Religious Mania may have been the original disease, but I do not think either hypothesis is likely. The murderer in external appearance is quite likely to be a quiet inoffensive looking man probably middle-aged and neatly and respectably dressed. I think he must be in the habit of wearing a cloak or overcoat or he could hardly have escaped notice in the streets if the blood on his hands or clothes were visible.

Assuming the murderer to be such a person as I have just described he would probably be solitary and eccentric in his habits, also he is most likely to be a man without regular occupation, but with some small income or pension. He is possibly living among respectable persons who have some knowledge of his character and habits and who may have grounds for suspicion that he is not quite right in his mind at times. Such persons would probably be unwilling to communicate suspicions to the Police for fear of trouble or notoriety.

Of course, with the killer still at large and unavailable for study nobody knew whether Bond's deductions were accurate or not.

As yet the state of the body of Mary Kelly had not been made public. Witnesses talking to the press had confirmed that the abdomen had been cut open and that other mutilations had been inflicted on the body. Press and public alike were convinced that what had happened this time was worse than anything before, and awaited the inquest for the gory details. They were to be disappointed.

'THE EAR AND EYES...ARE ALL I CAN RECOGNISE'

On 12 November the inquest was held in front of Dr Macdonald, MP, the coroner for the North-Eastern District of Middlesex. One of the first witnesses was Joseph Barnett, who had identified the body as being that of his long-term lover Mary Kelly. Some indication of the horror found in the room in Miller's Court came when he was asked by the coroner if he had formally identified the body. He replied: 'I have seen the body, and I identify it by the ear and eyes, which are all that I can recognise.' For this to be the case the body had obviously been treated even worse than that of Catherine Eddowes.

After hearing from witnesses who had found the body or who lived in Miller's Court, the court fell quiet as Dr George Phillips took the stand. After explaining how he had been called to the scene of the crime he continued:

> On the door being opened it knocked against a table which was close to the left-hand side of the bedstead, and the bedstead was close against the wooden partition. The mutilated remains of a woman were lying two-thirds over, towards the edge of the bedstead, nearest the door. Deceased had only an under-linen garment upon her, and by subsequent examination I am sure the body had been removed, after the injury which caused death, from that side of the bedstead which was nearest to the wooden partition previously mentioned. The large quantity of blood under the bedstead, the saturated condition of the palliasse, pillow, and sheet at the top corner of the bedstead nearest to the partition leads me to the conclusion that the severance of the right carotid artery, which was the immediate cause of death, was inflicted while the deceased was lying at the right side of the bedstead and her head and neck in the top right-hand corner.

He then fell silent and was asked no questions about the mutilations or the autopsy.

Instead Inspector Abberline took the stand to give details of the investigation to date. The coroner then asked, 'Is there anything further the jury ought to know?'

Abberline replied, 'No; if there should be I can communicate with you, sir.' Clearly he did not want the real horrors of the room to be made public. The jury promptly returned a verdict of 'murder against some person or persons unknown'.

LYNCHING MOBS ON THE LOOSE

The police certainly had reason to try to avoid inflaming the situation. Ever since the body had been found there had been large crowds in and around Dorset Street as Whitechapel residents gathered to exchange news, peer into the entrance to Miller's Court and speculate about the killings. At times more than a thousand people were present. On the evening of 11 November the sky cleared and a full moon was seen. There was immediate gossip around the crowd that the killer was a lunatic, a madman influenced by the waxing of the moon who would suffer his worst bouts of madness at the full moon.

At that moment some men at the back of the crowd spotted a man dressed in a most peculiar fashion. He had on good quality boots and trousers, over which he had put a threadbare, poor quality jumper – and he had blacked his face though not his hands as if to resemble one of the black sailors who came from the ships in the port. The men demanded to know who he was, but the man sought to slip away. He was promptly grabbed amid much shouting and jostling. The man tried to break free, and was rewarded with punches, kicks and blows.

'He is the Ripper!' arose a shout and a rope appeared from somewhere.

The man was being jostled towards a lamppost, apparently to be lynched, when the policemen who had been guarding the entrance to Miller's Court decided to take a hand. Wading through the crowd they shouted that people must clear the way for the Queen's Uniform, and struck out with truncheons at those who did not move fast enough. More policemen who had been round the corner in case of some such disturbance then ran into the crowd from the Commercial Street end. Between them the two groups of policemen managed to get hold of the man. By now so badly battered he could barely stand, the man was half carried, half marched to Leman Street Police Station. The mob followed in full cry, with shouts of anger and cries for justice. For more than an hour they stayed outside, shouting that the Ripper should be handed over to them.

The man was locked up in the cells and a doctor called. He turned out to be a gentleman from a smart area of the West End who had thought his 'disguise' would allow him to mingle in the East End to view the murder scenes without attracting attention. He was held overnight while the police checked out his story, then taken home under escort.

CHARLES WARREN REPLACED

With murderous mobs on the loose, it is no wonder the police tried to dampen down the horror of the situation. And the police had problems of their own. Sir Charles Warren, the commissioner of the Metropolitan Police, had just resigned. Warren had been in the post for just two years, and had already fallen out with the Home Secretary, Henry Matthews, over police organization. The public had largely turned against him over his actions in November 1887. A large demonstration of about 10,000 had gathered in Trafalgar Square to demand the release of left-wing MP William O'Brien, who was in prison for his role in organizing a demonstration in Ireland. The police were patrolling the demonstration, but as the situation turned rough Warren sent in 400 infantry with fixed bayonets. In the ensuing fighting three people were killed and 200 hospitalized.

Unpopular with both his employer and the public, Warren felt himself to be under attack from the newspapers over his failure to catch Jack the Ripper. He responded with a bluntly worded diatribe that was published in a London magazine. The article had been written and published without the permission of the Home Secretary. Warren was told to report for an official reprimand, but resigned instead. He was replaced by James Munro, up to that point the head of the CID at Scotland Yard. It was a bad time for the police to be short of leadership, but Munro at once set about the task of tracking Jack the Ripper.

THE SCARES AND ALARMS CONTINUE

On 13 November another dead woman was found at Wapping, half a mile south of Whitechapel. This time the body was found floating in the River Thames. She was very well dressed and clearly a different sort of woman from those killed by the Ripper. As the police investigated, however, it turned out she was not that different. Before nightfall they had identified the woman as Frances Annie Hancock, who had been reported missing on 21 October by her landlady. The landlady helpfully provided the information that 32-year-old Mrs Hancock was each week given £5 in gold by a very well dressed gentleman who visited her regularly. Rather less helpfully she did not know the man's name, but did make it clear to the police that he was not Mrs Hancock's husband though he did know the dead woman most intimately.

The police took only a few days to find the gentleman in question: Mr Frank Pain of the Strand. At first he denied knowing Mrs Hancock, but after detailed questioning admitted to having a relationship with the

The Trafalgar Square riot of November 1887 saw the police pitched against socialists and Irish demonstrators. Three demonstrators died in the fighting.

woman. He said he had last seen her on 22 October when she had waved him goodbye at Liverpool Street Station as he went away on business for a few days. By this time the police were convinced Mrs Hancock had killed herself, but there was no solid evidence. The subsequent coroner's inquiry ended with a verdict of 'found drowned'.

On the same day that the body of Mrs Hancock was found, the police announced that those who lived or worked in Miller's Court would now be allowed back to their rooms. Nobody else was to be allowed entrance and two burly constables stood guard to enforce the rule. Room No. 13 remained locked. The crowd in Dorset Street was now smaller, barely 200 strong at its largest.

Meanwhile, more arrests were being made. An Irish sailor named Thomas Murphy was arrested on 14 November after he was seen to have a knife under his jacket. Another man was arrested at Spitalfields Market the same day at 2 am after he approached a woman and tried to induce her to go with him into a dark alleyway. The woman was suspicious and summoned a policeman. The man refused to give his name and address, saying he did not want his parents to know what he was up to. He was arrested and locked up until he did give the information. A third man was arrested in Dorset Street at around 3 am after the constables on duty at the entrance to Miller's Court saw him acting suspiciously. A fourth man was arrested in York Road after blurting out in a pub that he was Jack the Ripper. The other drinkers in the pub pounced on him and held him down while one man ran outside to get a policeman. All four men were released after being cleared by inquiries.

A rather different arrest took place just before midnight on 16 November when a man ran into the Commercial Street Police Station in a state of some excitement. Hard on his heels came a crowd of about 30 men shouting that he was Jack the Ripper and had attacked two women. The man begged the police for protection from the mob. He said his name was Wolf Leviehne and that he had been walking home to Tottenham after conducting some business in Whitechapel when he was approached by two women who asked if he was interested in sex. Leviehne had refused, whereupon one of the women shouted out, 'You are Jack the Ripper!' This had brought men running. Leviehne had tried to explain, but the men were in an ugly mood so he had fled to the nearest police station.

The sergeant on duty calmed the crowd by telling them that Leviehne would be held in custody to be investigated. He then sent men out to fetch the two women, Mary Johnson and Christine de Grasse, for questioning and then arrest. Next day the two women were charged in the magistrates' court with soliciting. Magistrate Bushby made it clear that while they were clearly guilty he was giving them an especially heavy penalty of 14 days in prison to deter others from making similarly wild and potentially dangerous accusations.

Over the days that followed there were more scares and alarms. Chalk writing appeared in Bermondsey signed 'Jack the Ripper' and promising, 'Dear Boss – I am going to do three more murders'. At Blackfriars Railway Station a man answering the description given by Hutchinson of the man he saw with Kelly was set upon by a crowd of men and escaped by jumping on to a train. On 19 November the remains of Mary Kelly were laid to rest. The *Evening News* reported:

> The funeral of the murdered woman Kelly took place at the Roman Catholic Cemetery, Leytonstone, this afternoon, the remains being removed thither from the Shoreditch mortuary. Large crowds were present. Three large wreaths were on the coffin, which bore the inscription, 'Marie Jeanette Kelly, died November 9, 1888, aged 25 years.' The car was followed by two mourning coaches.

Another chapter in the career of the killer known as Jack the Ripper was over. But the horror went on.

CHAPTER 10:

THE HORROR CONTINUES

The murder of Mary Kelly brought the death count up to seven since the spring and there was still no sign the killer had had enough. Extensive house-to-house searches were conducted in the wake of the brutal slaying. On the very day after Mary Kelly was buried screams rang out again in Whitechapel and a woman claimed to have been attacked by Jack the Ripper. The East End braced itself for more bad news as the killings looked set to go on and on

A MANHUNT IS CALLED OFF

The newspapers on the morning of 20 November carried details of the funeral of Mary Kelly, the latest arrests and other news linked to the Whitechapel murders. At the common lodging house at 19 George Street, Spitalfields, the manager and some residents were in the ground floor kitchen poring over the reports. It was just after 9 am.

Suddenly the peace was shattered by a terrible scream from upstairs. Moments later a man rushed down the stairs and out of the front door, turning towards Thrawl Street. Just after that Annie Farmer, a regular at the lodging house, staggered into the kitchen clutching her neck, which was gashed and bleeding badly. 'The Ripper,' she gasped. 'The Ripper.' She was wearing nothing but her bloodstained shift.

Things then moved fast. The manager ran to a downstairs room where a woman named Esther Hall was sleeping. He roused her to come to care for Farmer, then ran out to get a doctor. The other men in the kitchen had meanwhile set off in pursuit of the fleeing man. He had been dressed in a dark suit, wore a hard felt hat and sported a black moustache. They got to Thrawl Street, but could not see him. Giving other men the description of the wanted man, they spread out gathering more and more men as they did so. Soon a vast area of Whitechapel was seething with men searching for the mystery attacker. Before long the rumour had spread that Farmer was dead, a new victim of Jack the Ripper.

Meanwhile, Mrs Hall had been washing the wound on Mrs Farmer's neck. It proved to be neither deep nor serious, though it had bled profusely. Hall bound a strip of cloth around the neck for a bandage. She asked Farmer if she knew the man who had attacked her. Farmer replied, 'Yes; I was with him about twelve months ago, and he ill used me then.' She said that the man had got her drunk. When the doctor arrived he said the wound was not serious, but recommended a few days' rest in the workhouse infirmary and sent for a stretcher.

When the police arrived in George Street they diverted the stretcher carrying Farmer to Commercial Street Police Station so that the woman could be questioned. They also sealed off the room where the assault had taken place and left two constables on the door. It was as well that they did so for while some men were joining the search for the supposed murderer, others had dashed to George Street to view the scene and get the latest news. Others had gone to Commercial Street Police Station, and a crowd of about 200 was gathered there demanding news about the 'murder'.

A little before noon the police began distributing a handbill which read:

Wanted, for attempted murder, on the 21st inst., a man, aged 36 years; height, 5ft. 6in.; complexion dark, no whiskers, dark moustache; dress, black jacket, vest, and trousers, round black felt hat. Respectable appearance. Can be identified.

But even as the description was being circulated some policemen were having second thoughts. Farmer had a bad reputation in Whitechapel and it was suspected that she was not telling the truth about the apparent assault.

A search of the room had revealed some coins scattered about. A witness who had been just outside the lodging house when the man fled testified that he had said, 'What a — cow' as he came out. He had then begun to walk off before the cry of 'Ripper!' rang out, at which point he had run. There were also inconsistencies in Farmer's story. She had told Mrs Hall that she knew the man, but told the police she did not. She told the police that the man had picked her up in a pub and got her drunk before taking her back to the lodging house. The manager of the lodging house said that Farmer and the man had arrived at 7.30 am and that both were sober. The man had paid for a double room for them both for a full day. He had assumed that Farmer, who he knew to be a prostitute, had got a client. There were also questions about the wound. The police surgeon thought it could have been self-inflicted.

Taken together, the police thought the evidence pointed to Farmer being the criminal, not the victim. They believed that having had sex with her client she had sought to rob him, perhaps threatening to stab herself and claim that he was Jack the Ripper if he did not pay up. The man had refused and fled. The manhunt was called off.

ARREST FOLLOWS ARREST

It was not long before another manhunt was on again. At 1 am on 21 November a policeman on his beat heard a woman scream and ran towards the sound. He found a woman in a state of terror and a man running off towards Brick Lane. Blowing his whistle to summon assistance the policeman gave chase. After some minutes, the man ran into a policeman coming the other way and after a short struggle was subdued. The affair turned out to be a fairly prosaic street robbery with no link to the murders.

Late on the evening of 23 November Ellen Worsfold met a man on Westminster Bridge and took him back towards her rented rooms in Waterloo Road. As they approached the front door, the man produced a knife and stabbed her. He then ran off, while Worsfold screamed for help. A man living nearby called Jim Peters heard the screams and gave chase, wrestling the man to the ground and beating him into submission. A patrolling policeman then arrived and took the man into custody while sending for a doctor to attend Worsfold. The man turned out to be Collingwood Fenwick, who was known to the police following previous convictions for fraud and forgery. He was at first charged with attempted murder, but after the wound had been dressed this was changed to wounding. He was found guilty and jailed.

Another arrest took place on 27 November when a man picked up a prostitute in Whitechapel and took her to a pub for a drink. A group of men in the pub thought he resembled the description of the man seen with Kelly on the night she died. They sent for a policeman who arrested the man. He was later able to prove he had not been in London when Kelly was murdered and was let go. Another arrest in a pub took place on 1 December in the Crystal Tavern, Mile End. The suspect this time had attracted attention by being a stranger and by pestering a woman who did not want to talk to him. Once at the police station he gave a false name and address, later changing it to his real one when he realized he was a suspect in the Whitechapel murders. He too was released after giving a firm alibi.

By the middle of December the tension on the streets had begun to ease. The cold weather kept most people indoors, unless they were on their way somewhere. The large numbers of people hanging about chatting who had quickly made up crowds and vengeful mobs in the milder autumn evenings were no longer in evidence. Nor were drunks or prostitutes about on the streets so much. The horrors of the Jack the Ripper murders were still fresh in everyone's minds, but as the weeks passed and no new murder took place the public returned to something like their normal ways of life.

One incident in Dalston Lane, Hackney, stands out because of its rarity. A man clearly the worse for drink was staggering about. He lurched up to a woman and made a lewd suggestion to her. She turned her back and walked off at which the man shouted after her, 'I'll get you. I am Jack the Ripper!' Unfortunately for the man he was so drunk he had not noticed a patrolling policeman approaching. He was at once arrested and charged with being drunk and disorderly. When brought to court next day he was revealed to be Captain William Moses, a retired army officer of unblemished record and reputation. The magistrate remarked, 'For a man of your education and position to be guilty of such conduct is positively disgraceful. I will impose a fine of 40 shillings, with 7 shillings and sixpence for the doctor's fee, or one month in prison. I am not sure that I ought not to send you to prison without the option of a fine.'

On 13 December the city was momentarily excited when a policeman patrolling Lavinia Grove, King's Cross, found a human arm lying in the gutter. It did not take the police long to trace the limb as one missing from the anatomy class of a London hospital and they blamed a medical student for the prank.

MORE BODIES BUT THE RIPPER RULED OUT

More serious was the discovery made by Police Sergeant Robert Golding at 4.15 am on the morning of 20 December. He was patrolling along Poplar High Street when he glanced into the stable yard belonging to builder George Clarke. He saw a woman lying beside the boundary wall. Golding hurried over and found the woman was dead, although her body was still slightly warm to the touch. There were no obvious injuries, but the left leg was drawn up and aside as in the women killed by Jack the Ripper. Golding inspected the yard for signs of a struggle, but there were none and the only footprints were those of himself and the woman. He then summoned a constable to guard the body, and went off to report his find.

There was nothing on the body to identify the woman, but the presence of money in her pocket indicated that if she had been murdered then robbery had not been the motive. Golding well knew that the yard was used by street prostitutes to ply their trade as it was always unlocked and was quiet and out of the way. He also vaguely recognized the dead woman as being one such prostitute, but she was not a regular to the area and he did not know her name. The usual door-to-door questioning took place and turned up a local man, Thomas Dean, who had walked past the yard just after midnight and who was certain there had been no body there then.

The post-mortem next day failed to produce a clear cause of death, but there was a mark around the rear of the neck that might have been made by a cord being pulled tight. Dr Harris was of the opinion that the woman had been strangled.

The police then rounded up some prostitutes known to work Poplar High Street and took them to the mortuary to view the corpse. One, Alice Graves, identified the body as that of a woman she knew as 'Fair Alice', and thought her surname was Downey. She said that she had seen Alice at 2.30 am on the night she died drinking with two men she took to be sailors in The George in Commercial Road, Whitechapel. Most of the prostitutes agreed that Alice was probably in Poplar to avoid the hunting grounds of the Ripper.

Meanwhile, Dr Thomas Bond had gone to Poplar to view the body. More experienced in violent death than was Dr Harris, Bond decided that the marks on the neck were not consistent with strangulation by a cord. None of the other usual marks of strangulation were present. He thought the woman had choked to death, perhaps after having collapsed while drunk.

The identification of the body as belonging to Alice Downey proved not to be quite as straightforward as it seemed. It soon became clear that 'Alice Downey' was a false name used by the woman when working as a prostitute. It took the police a few days to find the right person to ask, but on 26 December it was finally ascertained that the dead woman's real name was Catherine Rose Mylett and that her family lived in Pelham Street. Two detectives were sent to break the news to the Myletts. They found the Mylett family throwing a party to celebrate Christmas with neighbours. They took Mrs Mylett aside and told her of her daughter's fate, whereupon the woman collapsed in a fit. Later that day she visited the mortuary and formally identified the body as that of her daughter.

The inquest was held under Wynne Baxter and saw the doctors disagree openly about the cause of death. Assistant Commissioner Robert Anderson also attended and stated that there was no evidence in the yard of any violence. He summed up by saying that there were no indications at all that the woman had been killed. The jury, however, found that Mylett had been murdered. Anderson was forced to accept the verdict and so the death was put down as a murder, but since he himself thought the death was due to natural causes he did not assign anyone to investigate the case.

With the new year of 1889 came a gradual slackening of terror in the East End. There had been no new murders, while the flow of letters, chalk writing and other peripheral matters had dried up. The Whitechapel Vigilance Committee found that subscriptions from local businesses had also dried up and while it met now and then its regular patrols ceased as there was no longer the money to pay for them.

On 2 June 1889 a pregnant Soho prostitute named Elizabeth Jackson went missing. Over the next 12 days the various parts of her body were found floating in the Thames, having been cut up with some skill into 17 pieces. The immediate suspect was the man with whom she lived, John Faircloth, who was missing. He turned up in Devon where he had gone some weeks earlier and had numerous witnesses to prove he had been there all the time. Police suspected that Jackson may have died during or as a result of a bungled abortion, but they had no proof. No killer was ever caught.

THE BODY OF ALICE MCKENZIE IS FOUND

At 12.50 am on the morning of 17 July PC Walter Andrews entered Castle Alley, just off Whitechapel High Street, while patrolling his usual beat. He had been round the circuit several times already that night, most recently passing down Castle Alley at about 12.20 am. He noticed a woman lying behind a cart and went over to find that she was dead. Her throat had been cut, her skirts lifted up and slash wounds inflicted on her abdomen. He began blowing his whistle to summon help, but then saw a man walk past the end of the alley. Andrews called him over and told him to guard the body while he went to get help. Running into Whitechapel High Street blowing his whistle, Andrews saw Sergeant Badham running towards him. Badham sent Andrews back to guard the body while he ran off to fetch help. On his way to the police station he also blew his whistle, summoning three other constables and sending them to help Andrews. At the station he found Inspector Edmund Reid, who brought Dr George Phillips with him to the scene. Reid and Phillips arrived at about 1.10 am.

By 2 am Commissioner of Police Munro was on the spot and taking command of the situation. He sealed off the entire area, and had men knocking on nearby doors to rouse residents to ask them questions. The local beat policemen were also summoned and asked if they knew the dead woman. They knew her by sight as being a local woman but none knew her name. Some thought she was a prostitute, others thought she was not. He next sent men to fetch the managers and wardens of all the common lodging houses in the area to come and see the body.

This led the police to a lodging house in Gun Street, Spitalfields, run by a Mrs Elizabeth Ryder. She pointed them to a resident named John McCormack whose wife had gone missing. McCormack was taken to view the body and identified it as Alice McKenzie, the woman with whom he was living as husband and wife although the two were not actually married.

The coroner's inquiry was held under Wynne Baxter on 18 July, by which time the police had put together a reasonably clear picture of both the dead woman's background and her movements on the night of her death. She had been born in Peterborough in 1849 and had moved to London in 1874. She had been married and had a son, who had moved to the USA sometime before 1883 when she met John McCormack. McCormack was an Irishman who had been invalided out of the army on a pension after the Crimean War. He earned extra money working as a messenger, porter and general helper to some tailors in Hanbury Street. McKenzie worked as a laundress and cleaner in some businesses in Spitalfields but occasionally went out to earn money as a street prostitute. McCormack said he disapproved of this and that McKenzie had not done so recently.

The couple had moved into Gun Street in April, renting a double room in a superior sort of lodging house that did not have dormitories. On 16 July McCormack got home from work, having stopped for a drink on the way, and lay down to rest as he was tired. He gave McKenzie money for the week's rent plus a shilling to spend as she liked. She took

Alice McKenzie had her throat cut in July 1889, but she is not today thought to have been a Ripper victim.

a local blind boy named George Dixon to the music hall for the afternoon show, returning to Gun Street about 8 pm. Dixon remembered that McKenzie had spent some time chatting to a man who bought her at least one drink. Mrs Ryder, who met McKenzie when she returned, thought she seemed slightly the worse for drink. At 8.30 pm McKenzie left Gun Street.

At 11.40 pm she was seen by a friend, Margaret Franklin, who was chatting to a couple of other women in Flower and Dean Street. McKenzie was walking quickly towards Brick Lane. Franklin called out a greeting and McKenzie replied, 'I'm all right. I can't stop now,' and hurried on. There were no further sightings of her until her body was found.

McKenzie was not the only woman missing from Gun Street. A younger woman named Margaret Cheeks had gone out the same evening and not come back. The police circulated her description and began searching for her. Two days later she reported to a police station, having gone to visit her sister.

WAS THE RIPPER RESPONSIBLE?

All this was reported at the inquest, but as before it was the doctor's testimony about the state of the body that the press and the public were waiting for. The full extent of the mutilations to the body of Mary Kelly had still not been made public, though they were known from witnesses who had seen the body to have been horrifically extensive. When Dr Phillips took the stand at the inquest into Alice McKenzie, Coroner Baxter began by stating, 'There are various points that the doctor would rather reserve at the moment.'

Phillips then reported that death had been caused by two stab wounds to the left side of the neck, one of which had severed the main artery. These wounds seemed to have been inflicted when the victim was already lying on the ground. There were then several other wounds including a seven-inch long shallow wound from the bottom of the left breast to the navel along with seven or eight scratches running for two inches or so downwards from the navel. There were also several large bruises to the upper chest. Phillips thought that the killer had held McKenzie down with one hand on the chest while he had stabbed her with a knife in the other hand. Having heard the evidence, Baxter adjourned the inquiry to 14 August.

When the court reconvened it was to hear from Dr Phillips again, presumably giving the details that had been deliberately held back before. He spoke for only about ten minutes and the key exchange began with a question from Coroner Baxter:

Coroner: Are the injuries to the abdomen similar to those you have seen in the other cases?

Witness: No, Sir. I may volunteer the statement that the injuries to the throat are not similar to those in the other cases.

Behind the scenes the question of whether McKenzie had been killed by Jack the Ripper or not had been dividing the police. Dr Thomas Bond thought that she had been, stating:

I see in this murder evidence of similar design to the former Whitechapel murders, viz. sudden onslaught on the prostrate woman, the throat skillfully and resolutely cut with subsequent mutilation, each mutilation indicating sexual thoughts and a desire to mutilate the abdomen and sexual organs. I am of opinion that the murder was performed by the same person who committed the former series of Whitechapel murders.

Commissioner Munro agreed, but Assistant Commissioner Anderson and Inspector Abberline did not. The murder of McKenzie proved to be a short-lived sensation in Whitechapel. After several days of excitement on the streets normal daily life resumed. The excitements and alarms of the previous autumn did not return. Mobs did not pounce on oddly dressed passers-by and try to lynch them, men were not attacked in pubs and the police did not arrest anyone seen acting strangely. The rest of the year passed quietly. Whoever Jack the Ripper had been and whatever his motives, he seemed to have stopped killing. There were no more murders in Whitechapel and, although the area remained a violent one where crime was rife, women could walk the streets with a reasonable expectation of living to get home safely.

HAD THE CONSTABLE MISSED JACK THE RIPPER?

But there was to be one more murder in Whitechapel before the horror ended. As with McKenzie, opinion at the time was divided as to whether this was the work of the unknown murderer who went by the name of Jack the Ripper or not.

On the night of 12/13 February 1891 PC Ernest Thompson was patrolling his beat around Prescott Street and Leman Street. This was a complex area to patrol as it lay adjacent to Fenchurch Street railway station and had numerous yards, courtyards and alleyways. To make it even more difficult, the railway lines were raised up on a series of brick arches, some of which were used for storage while others were thoroughfares and some were closed up as sheds. Swallow Gardens was one such long railway arch used by carts to cross from one side of the lines to another. The stable yard used by carts servicing the railway station goods yard was about 100 yards away and was busy at all hours.

As Thompson turned into Swallow Gardens at 2.15 am with his measured tread he heard a man walking briskly away from him. Seconds later Thompson saw a woman lying on her back in the road. She opened an eye to look at him, then closed it again. Thompson dashed to her side, saw blood oozing from her neck by the light of his lamp and blew his whistle for assistance. He said later that he wanted to chase after the man whose footsteps he had heard, but decided instead to stay with the injured woman. It was a decision that would haunt him for the rest of his life. The woman's injuries were fatal, and he always worried that by mere seconds he had missed arresting Jack the Ripper.

Within the next five minutes Thompson had been joined by PC Fred Hyde and Detective George Elliott, both of whom had heard his whistle and had come running. Hyde went off to fetch a local doctor, returning with Dr Frederick Oxley who pronounced the woman to be dead. He found that the woman's throat had been cut, so it was obviously murder. By this time workmen from the railway stable yard had appeared and were questioned. One of them said that he had seen the dead woman with a man talking near the entrance to Swallow Gardens at about 1.30 am. He described the man as 'being above the middle height, and having the appearance of a foreigner, after the style of a ship's fireman'.

FRANCES COLES WALKS TO HER DEATH

Inspectors Donald Swanson and Henry Moore were sent for and they arrived an hour or so later, followed as day broke by Robert Anderson and Melville Macnaghten, the recently appointed Chief Constable. Swanson sent a message to the River Police asking them to visit every ship in the port of London, starting with those due to leave that day, to search for a sailor matching the description given by the railwayman.

The local beat police constables were summoned and promptly identified the dead woman as being a street prostitute who was widely known as Carroty Nell, but whose real name was either Frances Coles or Coleman. She moved frequently between various common lodging houses in and around Flower and Dean Street. Police visited all the lodging houses and found that Coleman had been staying in Thrawl Street. A fellow guest there, Samuel Harris, said that at about 9 pm the night she died Coles had been in the kitchen when a sailor came in and went straight up to her. He asked Coles if she had any money and on being told she did not he asked Harris if he would accept a ship's advance note (a promise to pay a sailor a proportion of his wages in advance of the ship sailing) for a bed for the night. Harris replied that he was a guest, not the manager, whereupon the sailor had then left. Harris said he thought the sailor looked drunk, and gave the police a description that vaguely matched that supplied by the railwayman.

The police at once spread out armed with the description of the suspect to visit every pub, café, lodging house and other likely site in the East End. Swanson and Harris were on hand so that Harris could view anyone who roughly fitted the description. At the Phoenix pub Harris positively identified a sailor named Thomas Sadler as being the man he had seen. Sadler was arrested and taken away for questioning.

The police then pieced together Coles' last couple of days. Sadler's ship called regularly at London and Coles was one of the prostitutes he sought out whenever in port. On this trip he had arrived on 11 February and had met Coles within hours. She had agreed to stay with him until his ship left. They spent that night at a lodging house in Spitalfields, then spent the next day drinking and strolling around east London. Sadler bought her a new hat for half a crown. At about 8 pm the two had an argument and split up. Sadler was later attacked in the street by two men and a woman who robbed him of his money. He then went to the lodging house where he knew Coles would be to ask her for some of the money he had given her. This was when he was seen by Harris. Coles said she had spent the money, and Sadler went off in a huff.

Sadler then went back to the docks to try to return to his ship, but was prevented by dock workers, whom he attacked with his fists. The dockers left Sadler bruised, battered and bleeding from a cut to his scalp. Sadler was seen by Police Sergeant Wesley Edwards near the Tower of London at about 2 am – this was only a five minute walk to the scene of the murder. Edwards noticed the sailor due to the blood on his face, and went over to check his wounds. Edwards judged the wound to be non-serious and though he thought Sadler to be very drunk he was not incapable so he let him be. At 3 am Sadler tried to get into a lodging house, but the manager threw him out for being drunk and belligerent. At 5 am Sadler stumbled into the London Hospital, where his head wound was patched up. He then went to the Sailors' Home in Wells Street to rest.

Coles, meanwhile, had slept for a while in the kitchen but had woken up at about 1 am when the manager, Charles Guiver, asked her to pay for a bed for the night or leave. She left and was next seen entering Shuttleworth's Eating House in Wentworth Street at about 1.30 am. She spent a penny ha'penny on a plate of cold mutton and bread, leaving again at about 1.45 am. She went east to Commercial Street then headed

Frances Coles was the last of the women to be counted among the Whitechapel murders, but was probably not a victim of the Ripper.

south towards the docks. There she met and chatted to a fellow prostitute named Ellen Calana.

Just as they parted, a man approached Calana. She did not like the look of him, so she refused to go with him. He punched her and moved off towards Coles. Calana called out, 'Frances, don't go with that man, I don't like his look.' Coles however called back that she would go with the man, so Calana added, 'If you are going with that man I will bid you goodnight.' She then continued to walk Commercial Street for a while before turning in for the night. She said that the last she saw of Coles she was walking south with the man, heading towards the spot where she would be murdered. Calana gave police a very good description of the man, but it was nothing like Sadler, being shorter, darker and wearing different clothes.

WAS IT THE RIPPER THIS FINAL TIME?

The autopsy showed that Coles had been thrown violently to the ground and her head punched back before her throat was cut. There were no other wounds. This seemed quite different from the way the victims of Jack the Ripper had been killed. However, she was a prostitute, her throat had been cut, the attack seemed motiveless, robbery was not a factor as she still had her money and it had taken place in Whitechapel. Again opinion in the police force was divided as to whether Coles was another victim of the Ripper.

Meanwhile, Sadler was charged with the murder. Edwards' evidence put him within five minutes' walk of the murder scene and some ten minutes before it took place. He had known the victim and was clearly drunk and aggressive. The case against him soon began to fall apart. At the coroner's inquest it became clear that the murder had been committed by a man who not only knew where the main artery was, but had been sober enough to cut it cleanly with the first cut. Sadler had been so drunk he could barely stand. The police dropped the charge and let Sadler go.

With the release of Sadler the story of Jack the Ripper drew to a close. There were to be no more murders, no more clues and no more arrests. The terror that had stalked the streets of Whitechapel sank back into the gloomy darkness of the London night from which it had emerged.

THE RIPPER IN RETROSPECT

It is more than a century since Jack the Ripper brought terror and murder to the streets of Whitechapel. The investigation at the time was as good and thorough as it could possibly have been, but with the benefit of hindsight more evidence has come to light in recent years that has allowed Ripperologists to put forward new theories and ideas about who was to blame and how the murders were actually committed.

VICTORIAN JACK THE RIPPER SPECULATION

The murders carried out by Jack the Ripper slowly faded from the minds of Londoners. As the months passed and no new murders took place the gruesome horrors slipped into the background. Everyone remembered, of course, but people had their livings to earn, children to care for and lives to lead. Gradually the East End of London slipped back to its normal pattern of daily life, much as it had been before Jack the Ripper began his deadly prowl through the streets.

But there were those who did not allow the memory of Jack the Ripper to disappear completely. Among them were the leading police officers who had investigated the murders. Most of them thought the 1891 murder of Frances Coles was not committed by the Ripper, nor that of Alice McKenzie in 1889. Clearly the killings had stopped and the police speculated as to why this might be. They came up with two answers. Either the killer had died or he had been locked up for some reason – either for some unrelated crime or due to insanity. The police began going over their files looking for someone who had died or been locked up soon after the Kelly murder in early November and who might have been the killer.

One result of this speculation was the document that has become known as the Macnaghten Memorandum of 1894. Melville Macnaghten had not joined the London police until after the killings – having previously been a police officer in India – but it fell to him to write the internal memo after newspapers pinned the blame for the Ripper murders on a young man who had been convicted of stabbing young women in the buttocks. The memo was for internal use only and was not made public until 1959. The purpose of the document was to establish the innocence of the man being blamed, but it also shed much light on opinion within the Metropolitan Police at the time. On the other hand it contained a number of factual inaccuracies and seems to have been written up hurriedly from memory without checking the relevant files.

Macnaghten stated that there were only five murders that could definitely be ascribed to the same man. These were the murders of Nichols, Chapman, Stride, Eddowes and Kelly. Most modern researchers follow Macnaghten, thus excluding the other murders of the time. This is odd for in 1888 Martha Tabram had been treated as a victim of the killer by everyone, and many had thought Emma Smith another victim. Certainly the Tabram murder had more similarities with what have become known as 'the canonical five' than differences. Some modern researchers think that the non-fatal attacks on Annie Millwood and on Ada Wilson may have been the work of Jack the Ripper. The attacks share features with the five murders, though as they did not result in death the police in 1888 did not link them to the later attacks.

Macnaghten went on to say that there were several men who may have been the killer, but he picked out three to demonstrate his point. These were:

(1) A Mr M. J. Druitt, *said to be a doctor & of good family – who disappeared at the time of the Miller's Court murder, & whose body (which was said to have been upwards of a month in the water) was found in the Thames on 31st December – or about 7 weeks after that murder. He was sexually insane and from private information I have little doubt but that his own family believed him to have been the murderer.*

(2) Kosminski – *a Polish Jew – & resident in Whitechapel. This man became insane owing to many years indulgence in solitary vices. He had a great hatred of women, specially of the prostitute class, & had strong homicidal tendencies: he was removed to a lunatic asylum about March 1889. There were many circumstances connected with this man which made him a strong 'suspect'.*

(3) Michael Ostrog, *a Russian doctor, and a convict, who was subsequently detained in a lunatic asylum as a homicidal maniac. This man's antecedents were of the worst possible type, and his whereabouts at the time of the murders could never be ascertained.*

There are several errors in this list. Druitt was a teacher, not a doctor, while Ostrog was imprisoned for fraud, not put in an asylum as a homicidal maniac. What emerges from the document is that the police believed that they knew the type of person they were looking for and even the area where he lived, but that they had no chief suspect.

This view is corroborated by the few statements made by other policemen involved in the case. Throughout the Ripper's reign of terror, the police kept their opinions and many facts secret. Nor were policemen then in the habit of writing autobiographies or talking to the press off the record. As a result there are only a few comments to go on.

Montague John Druitt committed suicide soon after the Kelly killing, at which point the killings ended.

Frederick Abberline was involved in the case from the very start. In 1903 he told a newspaper, 'Scotland Yard is really no wiser on the subject than it was fifteen years ago.' He went on apparently to dismiss two of the suspects on Macnaghten's list even though this list was not then public.

It is simple nonsense to talk of the police having proof that the man is dead. I know that it has been stated in several quarters that 'Jack the Ripper' was a man who died in a lunatic asylum a few years ago, but there is nothing at all of a tangible nature to support such a theory. Soon after the last murder in Whitechapel the body of a young doctor was found in the Thames, but there is absolutely nothing beyond the fact that he was found at the time to incriminate him.

Edmund Reid speculated in 1912 about the type of man responsible:

The perpetrator of the crimes was a man who was in the habit of using a certain public-house. The killer when drunk would leave with his victim and would in some dark corner attack her with the knife and cut her up. Having satisfied his maniacal blood-lust he would go away home, and the next day know nothing about it.

Clearly he had no particular man in mind.

Swanson wrote, 'The suspect was sent to Stepney Workhouse and then to Colney Hatch and died shortly afterwards.' This is clearly a reference to the Kosminski mentioned by Macnaghten, but Swanson agrees that the man was only a suspect and not certainly the killer.

VICTORIAN VS. MODERN CRIMINAL PROFILING

Given that Jack the Ripper was the first serial killer, in the modern sense, to find anonymity and cover in a large city it is interesting to compare the police record in 1888 with modern opinions. Serial killers are notoriously difficult to identify, even with the most modern techniques, so the fact that the London police did not catch Jack the Ripper does not necessarily count against them.

The profile of the likely killer drawn up by Dr Bond is very close to what modern offender profilers have concluded. In 1989 a group of FBI criminal profilers reviewed the evidence using the very latest theories and techniques, reaching broadly similar conclusions.

> *We would not expect this type of offender to be married. He would not be adept at meeting people socially and most of his heterosexual relationships would involve female prostitutes. He would be perceived as being quiet, a loner, shy, slightly withdrawn, obedient and neat and orderly in appearance when working. He would live or work in the Whitechapel area. The first homicide would be in close proximity to either his home or workplace. Investigators would have interviewed him during the course of the investigations. Investigators and citizens in the community would have had a preconceived idea of what Jack the Ripper would look like. Because of the belief that he must appear odd or ghoulish; the true Ripper would have been overlooked and/or eliminated as a possible suspect.*

Given that Bond had drawn a remarkably similar picture of the killer, the last conclusion may be considered incorrect.

The Whitechapel Vigilance Committee should also be given credit for concluding that the murderer lived in a comparatively small area north of Whitechapel High Street, east of Commercial Street and west of Middlesex Street. How they reached this conclusion is not known, but modern profilers have come to the same conclusion. Most serial killers commit their first murder close to their home or place of work, with later crimes taking place across a wider area but within a limited travelling time of their home or workplace. Tabram was killed in the centre of the area chosen by Lusk's committee, and the bloody apron of Eddowes was found there as well. It has been suggested that the apron was used to carry the organs removed from Eddowes' body back to the killer's room. The killer then went out a second time to throw away the apron and, perhaps, write the chalk message about the 'Juwes'. The later murders all took place within a small oval of territory that would take about 12 minutes to walk across and which centres on the same small group of streets.

HOW WELL DID THE VICTORIAN POLICE PERFORM?

Police efforts to catch the killer were focused on two basic ideas. The first was that the killer had previously met or known the victims. It was for this reason that they spent so much time tracing the background of the victims and interviewing people who had known them. This was a reasonable position for the police to take. Nearly all 19th-century murders were perpetrated by a killer known to the victim. The London police assumed the same would be the case, at least for the first couple of murders. After that they did begin to suspect that the killer chose victims at random.

Modern researchers have often derided the efforts the police put into researching the victims and their backgrounds. But they may not have been quite as misguided as some think. It is true that most serial killers choose victims that they do not know – choosing a victim that fits a certain look or appearance instead – but not all. The American serial killer John Gacy murdered at least 33 teenage boys during the 1970s. He was caught after he murdered the teenage son of a business contact.

Moreover there are hints that the victims may have known the killer, even if only briefly, before their fatal meeting with him. Each of the victims had a new trinket which they had not had the previous day. Nichols boasted about having a pretty new bonnet on the evening she was killed, Chapman was found with two farthings when she had previously been penniless, Stride's jacket sported a flower and fern buttonhole she did not have earlier in the day, Eddowes was found with a red leather cigarette case that she had not previously owned and Mary Jane Kelly was reportedly given a red handkerchief by a man seen with her shortly before her murder. Perhaps the killer used the services of the prostitutes on more than one occasion, giving them little gifts to win their confidence, before leading them to their deaths. If this were the case then the police may well have found Jack the Ripper by looking into the victims' pasts.

The other mainspring of the police efforts to catch the killer was the regular street patrols by constables, aided by the toughs employed by the Whitechapel Vigilance Committee. In part the patrols were intended to reduce the opportunities open to the killer to strike again. In this they were undoubtedly successful. The long gap between the 'double event' and the murder of Mary Kelly can perhaps be explained by the fact that there was simply no longer an opportunity for Jack the Ripper to have enough time to kill and indulge his cravings for mutilations before somebody would come by on patrol. The fact that Kelly was murdered indoors, not on the street, could be explained the same way. Frustrated in his attempts to murder outside, the killer instead opted to kill indoors.

But the patrols were also intended to catch the killer. Again there are modern parallels. Peter Sutcliffe is known to have murdered 13 women in northern England during the 1970s and 1980s, and may have killed more. He was caught when a policeman saw him acting suspiciously late at night in the driveway of an industrial premises. A quick check found that Sutcliffe was driving a car with false number plates, so he was arrested and taken in for questioning. It was only when he was searched and found to have a knife on him that the police thought he might be the long searched for 'Yorkshire Ripper'.

Another serial killer caught by a routine patrol was Ted Bundy, who killed between 30 and 40 women in America during the 1960s and 1970s. In 1975 his car was stopped as part of a routine traffic check by a Utah highway patrol officer. His car was found to contain tools commonly used by burglars, so he was arrested and questioned. It was not until some months later that the officers investigating Bundy for burglary and theft noticed the links to several unsolved murders.

Rather more dramatic was the arrest of British serial killer Donald Neilson in 1975. Two policemen stopped him late one evening when they saw him acting suspiciously. Neilson pulled a sawn-off shotgun from the bag he was carrying and fired, wounding one of the officers. The other ran to a nearby chip shop screaming for help. The men in the chip shop ran out, tackled Neilson and beat him so badly that he needed hospital treatment.

Clearly regular patrols that stop and question anyone acting oddly are a good method of catching criminals. Given that Jack the Ripper was operating in a fairly small area of London, the patrols had an even better chance of catching him. It was for this reason that the police constables made so many arrests during the autumn of 1888. Anyone and everyone behaving strangely was taken in so that the detectives could question them, sometimes for hours on end, then hold them while their stories were checked out.

Modern researchers believe that the police almost certainly did arrest and question Jack the Ripper at some point but that he managed to talk his way to freedom. Several more recent serial killers have likewise been questioned and released. British serial killer Fred West was imprisoned for theft as well as being arrested for rape, but released for lack of evidence, before his murders came to light.

Even so the police evidently came close to catching Jack the Ripper at least once. When Catherine Eddowes was murdered in Mitre Square the killer was almost certainly still with her body when PC Watkins entered the narrow alley that led from Mitre Street to Mitre Square. The sound of his footsteps alerted the killer to an approaching policeman, whereupon he fled. There were two other alleys out of the square – one led to King Street and the other to Duke Street. In Duke Street at that precise moment was PC Harvey who would not have failed to see anyone running out of the alley just as Watkins blew his whistle on discovering the body. By sheer chance the killer must have left by way of King Street. This was probably the closest the police ever got to catching the killer.

HOW WELL DID THE VICTORIANS KNOW THEIR MAN?

It would seem that the police eventually did get close to an accurate assessment of the type of man they were after and his motives for killing. As we saw in chapter 8, one medical expert wrote at the time:

> There can, however, be little doubt that in the Whitechapel atrocities we are brought face to face with...murder (and mutilation too) committed from purely voluptuous motives, the perpetrator being one of those strange individuals who are otherwise unable to obtain complete sexual gratification.

Mutilation in this context was said to refer to a situation 'in which the bowels and genital organs have been either simply excised, or carried away as well'.

The terminology is Victorian, but the assessment could have been produced today. The choice of victims may have been driven by the type of person the killer could get alone in secluded places, but the use of a knife and subsequent mutilations are now considered typical of serial killers driven by lust. The connection between murder, mutilation and sexual gratification is now accepted as fact.

A common trait among such lust killers is the way that the craving for satisfaction and the way this is carried out in fact escalates over time. This too is seen in the case of Jack the Ripper. The nature and scale of mutilations inflicted on the corpses became greater and more elaborate with each killing. The only exception was the murder of Elizabeth Stride, but the killer was clearly interrupted by the arrival of the cart driver Louis Diemschutz before he could carry out the desired mutilations. At the time the police held back from the public the true scale of the mutilations carried out on Mary Kelly, the last of the generally accepted victims. It was not until some years later that the details became public, and they demonstrate the lengths that Jack the Ripper went to when he had enough time. Whether he had intended to apply this sort of treatment to earlier victims, but had been interrupted, or whether he was building up to this level of violence is not clear.

According to Dr Bond's notes:

The whole of the surface of the abdomen and thighs was removed and the abdominal cavity emptied of its viscera. The breasts were cut off, the arms mutilated by several jagged wounds and the face hacked beyond recognition of the features. The tissues of the neck were severed all round down to the bone.

The viscera were found in various parts viz: the uterus and kidneys with one breast under the head, the other breast by the right foot, the liver between the feet, the intestines by the right side and the spleen by the left side of the body. The flaps removed from the abdomen and thighs were on a table.

The bed clothing at the right corner was saturated with blood, and on the floor beneath was a pool of blood covering about two feet square. The wall by the right side of the bed and in a line with the neck was marked by blood which had struck it in several places.

The face was gashed in all directions, the nose, cheeks, eyebrows, and ears being partly removed. The lips were blanched and cut by several incisions running obliquely down to the chin. There were also numerous cuts extending irregularly across all the features.

The neck was cut through the skin and other tissues right down to the vertebrae, the fifth and sixth being deeply notched. The skin cuts in the front of the neck showed distinct ecchymosis. The air passage was cut at the lower part of the larynx through the cricoid cartilage.

Both breasts were more or less removed by circular incisions, the muscle down to the ribs being attached to the breasts. The intercostals between the fourth, fifth, and sixth ribs were cut through and the contents of the thorax visible through the openings.

The skin and tissues of the abdomen from the costal arch to the pubes were removed in three large flaps. The right thigh was denuded in front to the bone, the flap of skin, including the external organs of generation, and part of the right buttock. The left thigh was stripped of skin fascia, and muscles as far as the knee.

The left calf showed a long gash through skin and tissues

to the deep muscles and reaching from the knee to five inches above the ankle. Both arms and forearms had extensive jagged wounds.

The right thumb showed a small superficial incision about one inch long, with extravasation of blood in the skin, and there were several abrasions on the back of the hand moreover showing the same condition.

On opening the thorax it was found that the right lung was minimally adherent by old firm adhesions. The lower part of the lung was broken and torn away. The left lung was intact. It was adherent at the apex and there were a few adhesions over the side. In the substances of the lung there were several nodules of consolidation.

The pericardium was open below and the heart absent. In the abdominal cavity there was some partly digested food of fish and potatoes, and similar food was found in the remains of the stomach attached to the intestines.

This was the last killing, and although the killer was never caught he did not murder again. It was speculated at the time that this may have been because he died or was locked away for some other reason. Another idea put forward was that in the Kelly killing the murderer had finally achieved satisfaction for his bloodlust by carrying out the hideous mutilations. Yet another theory was that the horrors of the final murder had driven the killer insane, leading either to his suicide or to his incarceration in a lunatic asylum.

Along with motivation for the killings, most serial killers have an established modus operandi (method of operation). Once they have found a way to kill a human with minimal risk to themselves that sates their cravings, serial killers tend to stick to it throughout their murderous careers. There have been exceptions, but Jack the Ripper does not seem to have been one of them. The police in 1888 were aware of this, and had clearly worked out what the MO was. Tabram was killed by a stab wound to the heart, with the abdominal mutilations apparently being carried out with a different knife. The later victims were all killed in a different way. The killer first gripped them tightly around the throat as if to strangle them. Once the victim was unconscious, but before they were dead, they were lowered gently to the ground whereupon the throat was slit to cut the artery and so to kill. It was the sudden throttling that accounted for the silence with which the Ripper operated. This first strike made the victims unable to utter a sound, while the gentle laying down meant that there was no noise made by the falling body.

MODERN ASSESSMENTS OF THE RIPPER SUSPECTS

One problem with assessing how well the police did in 1888 is that the vast majority of the official records were later thrown out during a routine clearing of out-of-date documents relating to past cases. Most of the official reports have survived, but the notebooks on which they were based have been lost. This means that much of the original evidence has been lost forever. Clues that the police may have overlooked due to an inexperience in dealing with serial killers, but which may have helped more modern researchers, are gone.

Similarly we know the conclusions that Abberline, Reid and others reached on various matters, but not why they reached them. We know that they considered Joseph Lawende to be a reliable witness and believed that his description of the man seen with Eddowes was almost certainly a true description of the killer. We know also that they thought George Hutchinson to be unreliable and so largely discounted his description of the man he saw with Mary Kelly. Why

Lawende was trusted but Hutchinson was not we have no idea. Modern researchers must either accept the views of the police of 1888 or discard them.

This lack of detailed evidence has not stopped modern researchers from putting forward their own ideas about how and why the killings took place. They have also put forward a wide-ranging list of suspects. These have included the three men put forward by Macnaghten.

Montague John Druitt

Montague John Druitt attracted attention because he committed suicide by drowning himself in the Thames about three weeks after the Kelly murder. There is nothing to link him to either the killings or to Whitechapel, and given that he was already suffering from nervous problems the reasons for his suicide are not hard to find. His father had recently died and his mother had been committed to a lunatic asylum while his grandmother had committed suicide and his sister had tried to do the same. Moreover he had just been fired from his job as a schoolmaster for undisclosed misdemeanours.

Aaron Kosminski

The Polish Jew 'Kosminski' mentioned by Macnaghten and by Swanson probably refers to Aaron Kosminski. Unfortunately most of the records relating to Kosminski after he had been confined for insanity have been lost. He seems to have suffered from paranoid schizophrenia and to have had hallucinations. The hatred of women mentioned by Macnaghten is not recorded elsewhere, but that is no reason to rule it out.

Michael Ostrog

The third Macnaghten suspect, Michael Ostrog, has recently been ruled out after records were found in France proving that he had been in prison there for fraud during August and September 1888. John Pizer and James Sadler, both suspected and then ruled out at the time, have been considered by some modern researchers to have been suspects, but they are generally dismissed.

David Cohen

David Cohen was another Whitechapel man who was incarcerated in a lunatic asylum soon after the death of Mary Kelly. In many ways the facts recorded by Macnaghten relating to Kosminski better match Cohen and it has been suggested that Macnaghten meant this man. Cohen was found wandering the street in a state of confusion in December 1888. At first he was taken to the workhouse but when he turned violent he was sent to the asylum at Colney Hatch. There he went through spells when he attacked fellow inmates and guards, as well as tearing off his clothes and smashing furniture. At other times he appeared to be quite normal. There are hints that he may have been suffering from tertiary syphilis. He died in October 1889.

Charles Cross

Several of the men who appeared as witnesses or as acquaintances of the victims have recently been suggested as having been Jack the Ripper.

One such was Charles Cross, the man who discovered the body of Mary Ann Nichols. Cross claimed that he was walking to work when he saw what he at first thought was a tarpaulin lying on the pavement. When he got closer he saw it was a woman, so he called out to another man to come over and look. The two men then went to find a policeman and tell him of their find. After giving their names and addresses they were allowed to go to work. However, the other man, Robert Paul, told a slightly different story. According to him, Cross had been standing for some time beside the body before he saw Paul and called him over. There was also a time problem as Cross had left his home at 3.20 am and was found by Paul at 3.40 am. Yet it is only a seven-minute walk from his home to the murder scene, leaving 13 minutes unaccounted for. Moreover the murder sites of both Tabram and Chapman, like that of Nichols, lie on the shortest walking route between Cross's home and his place of work. Counting against this is the fact that when asked by PC Jonas Mizen to give his name and address he did so. Neither Paul nor Mizen knew him by sight so he could easily have given a false name, but instead he gave his real one.

Joseph Barnett

Joseph Barnett, the estranged boyfriend of Mary Kelly, has also been put forward. His physical appearance matches reasonably well with that given by Lawende of the man seen with Eddowes – he was aged about 30, stood 5 feet 7 inches tall, had light brown hair, a moustache and was of medium build. He was known to drink ginger beer, while one part of the Dear Boss letter read, 'I saved some of the proper red stuff in a ginger beer bottle over the last job to write with.' If he were the killer it would explain the mystery of Kelly's locked door. It was locked when police arrived, so the killer either had a key or had reached through the window to lock it after he left the scene. Barnett had a key, and he knew it was possible to reach the lock through the open window. In addition, Barnett also fits well with the FBI profile of the Ripper. It has been suggested that he killed only Kelly for some private reason and then mutilated her body to make it appear that she had been killed by the Ripper. Against this is the fact that he was interviewed for several hours by Abberline, who then dismissed him as a suspect. The interview notes have been lost but Abberline is known to have checked out aspects of what Barnett told him independently. Abberline was certain Barnett was innocent, and he was there with access to much more information than we have.

George Hutchinson

George Hutchinson, apparently the last person apart from the killer to see Mary Kelly alive, is another modern suspect. He gave a very detailed description of the man he saw with Kelly, but the description does not tally with others of men who might have been the killer. He was also seen hanging about outside the murder scene barely an hour before the killing took place and so may have concocted his story to explain himself. On the other hand, he too was interviewed in detail by Abberline and dismissed as a suspect.

Neill Cream

Neill Cream was a serial killer who between 1891 and 1892 poisoned four prostitutes in London. When led to the scaffold for execution, Cream announced, 'I am Jack the. . .', at which point the lever was pulled and he died. It is rare, but not unknown, for a serial killer to change his MO. For some time it was thought that Cream may have changed from killing with knife in 1888 to killing with poison in 1891. However it has now been shown that he was in prison in Illinois in 1888.

Francis Tumblety

Slightly more exotic as a suspect is Francis Tumblety. This American fraudster and conman had a long and chequered career which involved him being in and out of prison, enjoying wealth and prestige, suffering periods of destitution and squalor and adopting a variety of names, titles and uniforms to which he was not entitled. He is recorded as having expressed a hatred of prostitutes on more than one occasion and was frequently violent when he did not get his own way. He is known to have been in Britain for most of 1888 and there is some reason to think he may have been the enigmatic Batty Street lodger. On the other hand he was homosexual and there are no known cases of a homosexual serial killer targeting women.

Walter Sickert

More outlandish suggestions made by recent authors have included the artist Walter Sickert. Sickert is known to have painted pictures of murders and murder scenes, and to have extensively used prostitutes as models. On the other hand most artists of this time used prostitutes as they were the only women who could be hired by the hour and were easily persuaded to get undressed or wear costumes. There is no known link between Sickert and Whitechapel.

Prince Albert Victor, Duke of Clarence

His Royal Highness Prince Albert Victor, Duke of Clarence, is perhaps the most high profile person to be put forward as a suspect. Eldest son of the Prince of Wales and so heir to the British throne, Clarence was always a bit of a wayward character. As a boy he did badly at education and there are hints that he may have been slightly retarded. He was

Walter Sickert painted images of violence against women that some think link him to the killings.

certainly lazy and shirked his duties whenever possible. He quarrelled with his parents and other members of the royal family and preferred the company of people generally deemed unsuitable for a future monarch. In 1889 the police raided a homosexual brothel in Cleveland Street in London. Homosexual acts were then illegal, and it soon became clear that some very rich and influential men had used the brothel. Among them was Lord Arthur Somerset, equerry to the Prince of Wales. It was rumoured at the time that Somerset had agreed to admit guilt to hide the identity of the true brothel client from the royal household, Clarence, though this has never been proved. Clarence died of pneumonia in 1892. It has been suggested that he fathered an illegitimate child with a pretty Catholic girl from the East End, and that the women were murdered either by Clarence or an agent to stop them telling the secret. There is no firm evidence for this theory.

James Maybrick

In 1992 a notebook turned up that seemed to be the handwritten diary of Liverpool businessman James Maybrick. The diary first attracted attention as Maybrick had died in 1889 from arsenic poisoning. His wife was found guilty in a sensational trial during which it was revealed that both she and James had committed adultery frequently and led very unorthodox lifestyles. Mrs Maybrick was later released on appeal. The diary had hidden within its pages details of the canonical five and two other murders that the writer, Maybrick, claimed to have committed. The diary was published in 1993 alongside the results of chemical tests that showed the paper and ink to be of 19th-century manufacture. However, the majority of researchers believe the diary to be a modern fake.

No doubt other names will be put forward, evidence for their guilt suggested and then disproved. It is most likely, however, that Inspector

James Maybrick was a Liverpool businessman who visited London frequently in 1888.

Abberline knew the truth back in 1888. The killings were committed by a local Whitechapel man who was inconspicuous because he was so perfectly normal most of the time. Like many other serial killers since he would have seemed quiet and inoffensive in his everyday life. He would have lived close to his first murder, exactly in the area where the police thought he lived. He would have moved easily through Whitechapel without attracting attention because he fitted in there perfectly.

But when the murderous bloodlust was upon him Jack the Ripper emerged to murder with unparalleled savagery, only to fade away again when the lust was sated.

INDEX

PICTURE CREDITS

Evans/Skinner Crime Archive: 39, 68, 80, 85, 95, 99, 106, 112, 120, 126, 146, 148, 153, 187, 190, 196, 198, 204, 217, 223, 229, 245, 247

Library of Congress: 17